ƒACTS
and
ƒANCIES

ALSO BY PAUL TAYLOR

Private Domain: An Autobiography

facts
and
fancies

Essays Written Mostly for Fun

PAUL TAYLOR

DELPHINIUM BOOKS
HARRISON, NEW YORK • ENCINO, CALIFORNIA

CONTENTS

FOREWORD

by Robert Gottlieb

No other dancer ever looked like Paul Taylor, that strapping, elastic, goofy hunk of a guy, and no one else's dance works look like his either—not like the deep, dark ones or the zany ones or the uplifting ones. His vocabulary, his tone are unique and unmistakable.

The same thing is true, it turns out, about his writing. His style is utterly his own, and like all real style it isn't a calculated voice but a reflection of the way his quirky mind works. He *couldn't* write any other way: No matter how hard he tried, it would still come out sounding like him.

This is an extraordinarily rare phenomenon among dance writers (among most writers). There was Agnes de Mille, who many people believe was a better writer than dancer or choreographer (I'm one of them). There's Allegra Kent, whose mind—like her dancing—goes its own sometimes wayward, always beautiful way; her autobiography, *Once a*

Dancer...., and the pieces she occasionally gives us, are like no one else's: personal, pointed, pointy, poetic.

Paul's autobiography, *Private Domain*, is like that too: personal, pointed, pointy—though not exactly poetic. Instead, he performs tricks, with his story and with us. He's a fabulist more than a historian, playing hide-and-seek with his feelings. Because he's honest, he tells us a lot, though far from everything, leaving us charmed, touched, and amused, even informed, but on shifting ground. The manner is so easy and good-natured that he almost manages to fool us into thinking he's really spilling the beans. But as with so many of his dance works, there's a loner Paul, standing apart, observing with us while pulling the strings.

Since I had the pleasure of being the editor of his autobiography, I was able to register how hard he worked, and how much writing meant to him; how he would stop in his tracks, backtrack, and struggle to make a sentence, a paragraph, a chapter better. He even welcomed editorial input—everything about the experience of being a writer excited and intrigued him. Most remarkable was how much he enjoyed doing it—at times I felt he resented having to stop work on the book in order to make a new dance, since it took him away from his desk.

Paul tells us he's a spy manqué, and you can see from the letters in this collection how carefully he's observing everyone around him—not only fellow-passengers but the crew. (Paul Taylor on a cruise?) He's tickled by the bizarre things that happen to him—like sitting on the Queen of England's hand, or going home, exhausted, from the premiere of Martha Graham's *Clytemnestra* to find an eviction notice in his mail. (Certainly Martha herself tickled him: "I...enjoy seeing her choreograph her body into snarls and then find such wonderful ways to get out of them.")

Spy, raconteur, but also—perhaps most of all—provocateur. Let's face it, when his dander is up he really likes sticking it to his target. There's his parody review of a dance performance by "Cleave Yarns." ("Already, even before the City Center curtain rose, the nerves in our toes began to tingle and the muscles in our abdomen started to knot.") There's the telephone interviewer from Hell—"Hello, this is Bethpage Bulova-Trit calling for the *San Bernardino Gazette*. Is this Paul Tylor?" Try to imagine his response to the following: "Please describe your Creative Process in detail."

The biggest tease is reserved for ballet (as opposed to Modern). Ballet, he assures us, "is just one dainty pose after another, see, is just a bunch of stiff necks, locked knees, and limp wrists...mostly done with the dancers looking over their shoulders as if admiring themselves in a mirror. Either that or making sure the audience is still there." (Sorry, Paul, this all sounds like pointe-shoe envy to me.) His great anti-ballet predecessor was Isadora Duncan, who the first time she traveled to Russia, the heart of the kingdom of ballet, told the great Russian dancers just what she thought of their art, to which they responded by embracing her and *her* art—just the way ballet company after ballet company around the world today embraces *Paul's* art. Talk about turning the other cheek!

There's a little bit of everything in this collection, including the opening chapters of a detective novel—*The Shirley Temple Murders*. How's this for the most succinct account of a character's death you've ever encountered: "Nudist camp, lightning." There's even serious stuff. His account of the birth of *Aureole* is partly light-hearted, yes, but more important, it's large-hearted and open-hearted: "What happened, and how *Aureole* felt to perform, are things that are nearly impossible for me to describe. To pare it down to basics: the curtain lifts, we depart from this world, find a far more vivid place, and then the curtain closes." This, to me, is wonderful writing. Finally, there is "Why I Make Dances," a completely serious response to a question there's no real answer for. Here, the reporter, the spy, the parodist, the provocateur disappear, and we get as close as we're ever likely to get, at least in words, to the "real" Paul Taylor. The important thing, though, isn't *why* he's made his masterpieces, but *that* he's made them. That he writes so well just adds to the mystery.

INTRODUCTION

by Suzanne Carbonneau

When asked to describe himself, Paul Taylor answers with a single word: "dancemaker." This is characteristically plainspoken of Taylor, who leaves it to others to assess the magnitude of his achievement. In the post-war era, when the United States emerged as the center of world concert dance, Taylor was hailed as America's shining son. Heir to the individualism of Isadora Duncan, the expressionism of Martha Graham, the formalism of George Balanchine, he parlayed this birthright into divine ambition: Taylor intended to create a world. And remarkably, he did just that. Taylor's choreographic universe teems with every kind of life—insects and heroes.

But dances are not the only things that Taylor makes. Taylor is a maker to his marrow. His waking hours are filled with creation—if he is not in the dance studio, he will be found concocting other things; he is a carpenter, gardener, sculptor, beekeeper, painter, tailor, costumer, animal husbandman. And as readers of this collection will discover, Taylor is also a writer. This is a startling turn for an artist who discloses that he choreographs because—as he writes in "Why I Make Dances"—"I don't always trust my own words."

A confessed loner, Taylor nevertheless has stayed in constant communication with the world, sending messages afloat in choreographic bottles. And writing is second only to dancemaking as his preferred mode of keeping in touch. But mostly, as in his choreography, he writes to tickle his own fancy, always game for a creative challenge.

In each new field he sets out to master, Taylor begins with craft, the edifice that has sustained his dancemaking. Taylor's choreographic poetics are the result of an unfettered imagination, certainly, but they are also embedded in know-how—in the mastery of spatial structure, dynamic contrast, rhythm and timing, musical expressiveness, and the semantics of posture and gesture. Taylor rules the rules, however; they do not rule him. He takes as much pleasure in flouting rules as in flaunting them.

Taylor has embraced writing with the same determination and discipline he applies to his choreography, and also the same sense of curiosity about how to achieve desired effects. Taylor has been known to pore, for sport, over style manuals and grammar tracts. And it is for sport that he then sets about giving the slip to these regulations. As in his cho-reography, he finds loopholes by adopting a distinctive—often, colloquial—voice. In "How to Tell Ballet from Modern," a manifesto disguised as farce, Taylor mugs Edward G. Robinson–style, wisecracking out of the side of his mouth: "Ballet is just one dainty pose after another, see, is just a bunch of stiff necks…" Or Taylor rummages through genres, heeding the get-out-of-jail cards that give each their peculiar flavor, dissecting their conventions and then freely burlesquing them. In this excerpt from *The Shirley Temple Murders*, he lampoons the hardboiled detective novel. But, as in his dances, he ransacks culture, high and low, for effects and references. The result? A screwball mash-up of everything from *Moby-Dick* to pulp fiction. In other words, vintage Taylor.

When Taylor set out to write his autobiography *Private Domain*, which was published in 1987, his aim was two-fold. He meant the book to be an exploration of his artistic coming-of-age—an attempt, it would seem, to explain himself to himself. But he also devised the project as a means to become adept at another art form. That he suc-ceeded is evident in the passages from *Private Domain* included here. As a reminder of just how accomplished a writer Taylor is, one need look no further than "Martha Close Up," his account of catching a first glimpse of Martha Graham. It is a marvel of vivid metaphor, wrought from penetrating observation and cunning analysis. His depiction of the choreographer's eyes alone—"there's something very wise and undomesticated in them, like the eyes of an oracle or an orangutan. That is, they look as if they've seen everything that's to be seen in the world. Maybe even more"—conveys more about the nature of Graham's artistry than have entire books written on the subject.

It is fascinating to plumb how closely his literary technique, tone, content, and style resemble what we find in his choreography. Taylor is famous for the variety of his dances, which can be musical abstraction, political satire, nature study, period gloss, slapstick, love story, gumshoe caper, elysian reverie, stygian nightmare—you name it. Their temperaments ricochet between beatific and unnerving, but in acknowledgment of the complexity of human experience, most of his dances are an amalgam of mood. In the same vein, Taylor has not cultivated one writing persona, but has unleashed a raft of voices in a raft of forms: travesty, comedy, fiction, essay, satire, allegory, poetry, fable, epistle. While many of these selections are humorous, as anyone familiar with Taylor's choreography knows, even in the sunniest of his dances, there are often threatening clouds on the horizon. And the canny Taylor recognizes when to swap his Janus masks for maximum emotional wallop.

For someone who has spent more than a half century in the public eye, Taylor has been adroit at largely disappearing from view. In *"Aureole,"* Taylor concedes that dancing the gut-busting technique he created was not his greatest challenge as a performer. Rather, it was self-disclosure that gave him the willies. In fact, he only did it once—the unadorned walk in silence that precedes his celebrated solo in *Aureole*. The simple action left him unmoored, feeling "stark naked." Taylor confesses, "The moment scares me to death."

For self-preservation, Taylor has adopted the guise of a Wizard of Oz, fronting for his Professor Marvel. As any wizard must, Taylor sports a bag of tricks to keep the rabble from peeking behind the curtain. "I make dances because crowds are kept at a safe distance, which is what proscenium stages are good for," he acknowledges in "Why I Make Dances." He steers the same course in his writing. The shape-shifting is camouflage against encroachment by audience, press, fans, even friends. "Having a name, being tagged and labeled," Taylor writes in "Two Bozos Seen Through Glass," "is a cage and not gilded." And if there is one thing that Taylor means to be, it is free. Art is where he hides, not where he reveals himself. Except when he does. Will the real Paul Taylor please stand up?

For Taylor, artifice is the basis of artmaking. Having spent a career transmuting life into art on the stage, Taylor does likewise on the page. Even in his writing, where autobiography is more clearly in evidence than in his dances, he prefers to apply lavish doses of imagination to the basic story. Taylor believes that there are some things that are more important than the puniness of facts, and there is nothing that can't be improved with artistic tinkering. "Recollections need to be somewhat choreographed," he advises in "*Aureole*." Typically in these pages, Taylor offers not veracity exactly, but a series of quasi-fabrications and near-accuracies—the method of a creative artist who understands how to shape a work so that what emerges is truthful, if not factual.

Taylor's ace-in-the-hole for hiding in plain sight is George H. Tacet, Ph.D., of Perth Amboy, a figment of his imagination given liberal rein in these selections. Tacet's role as alter ego is to keep Taylor in his place. For if Taylor has a horror greater than self-revelation, it is pretentiousness. While he has created some of the most sophisticated art of his time, Taylor has taken pains to live simply, avoid artists' cabals, shun affectation of any sort, and remain anchored in his working-class roots. The overly cultivated Tacet—full of humbuggery and empty of soul—is a cautionary tale. Without vigilance, any artist could find himself becoming a Tacet, and Taylor is always ready to pull the rug out from under the Tacet in him. Surely, there is nothing that Tacet would have loved more than being awarded the Légion d'Honneur. But when Taylor received the French government's highest honor, he wrote the satiric fantasy "In the Marcel Proust Suite of the Hotel Continental" to take himself down a peg. Here, Taylor not only bites the hand that feeds him—he can't help poking fun at the "frogs"—but he also sinks teeth into his own hide, caricaturing himself as a

Tacetian rube putting on the airs of a sophisticate. (Taylor is not the only one with a sense of humor. The French showed themselves good sports in having named Taylor a Chevalier, despite his having lobbed choreographic water balloons at them in his *Offenbach Overtures*.)

Tacet is, of course, the pseudonym Taylor has used in programs to disguise the fact that he has not always employed collaborators. It was Tacet who created the costumes for *Aureole* (and Taylor who takes credit for tearing off the gewgaws in Tacet's original designs). And it was Tacet who wrote an introduction for *Private Domain*, published here for the first time. It's less an introduction, actually, than it is a roast: Tacet takes the opportunity to berate Taylor for any number of sins, but mostly for disclosing so little of himself in the literary form designed for that purpose. Here, Taylor uses Tacet to have his cake and eat it too. In Tacet's voice, Taylor slyly lets it be understood that his evasions have been deliberate. He knows exactly what he is doing.

Although the facts may be hard to get at, still these selections can be revelatory of Taylor's choreographic character. And no one is harder on Taylor than he is on himself. In a fascinating excerpt from *Private Domain* about the creation of *Aureole* in 1962, Taylor divulges the crisis of conscience that took hold when the dance made him famous overnight. The popularity of *Aureole* "filled me with resentment," Taylor writes. "I was wary of it." The choreography had come quickly and easily, and it had not advanced his artistic goals as had other dances that "I had to dig for, grapple with, and slave over." Say, dances like *Epic*, which had rained infamy on him at its premiere just five years earlier. In "Two Bozos Seen Through Glass," Taylor looks back at this runt of his choreographic litter with compassionate reappraisal. A compendium of uninflected pedestrian postures, *Epic* had come close to ending Taylor's dance-making career just as it was beginning. Louis Horst—Martha Graham's factotum and the era's leading arbiter of modern dance—had notoriously damned Taylor without a word, his review nothing but a blank column. Writing 35 years after the creation of *Epic*, Taylor reconciles with the younger choreographic self who had spurned modern dance conventions. Offering a meditation on aesthetics, Taylor reminds us that artworks are "mysterious containers" that we read each in our own ways.

While Taylor cloaks many of his musings on art in jocular folksiness and low comedy, he has his say—Professor Marvel, in front of the curtain—in "Why I Make Dances." If life were fair and Nobel Prizes were awarded for choreography, Taylor would have been able to deliver this declaration of purpose as his acceptance speech in Stockholm. (As it is, he had to settle for its publication in the *Wall Street Journal*.) Taylor admits to writing the essay because he is frustrated by interviews—excruciating rituals he experiences on a near-daily basis—in which he has been asked every conceivable question. Every question, that is, except the only one that matters. Never mind. These indignities, satirized in "An Early Interview," goaded Taylor to drop the masks and speak from his heart about his artistic aspirations.

Taylor's friends know him as an inveterate and entertaining correspondent. Included here are letters that are exercises in genre (ghost story, travelogue, celebrity encounter), as well as ripping good yarns. There are also two true-crime stories, in which Taylor takes police matters into his own hands. It would seem that, for a recluse who lives a quiet life, Taylor has managed to have some hair-raising escapades. But, then again, he invites the mayhem, insisting that "I prefer to take care of interlopers myself." Taylor does exactly this in "The Strange Story of How I Chased and Caught the Guy Who Burgled My House," improvising a citizen's arrest by stuffing the thief into the trunk of a passing car.

Other selections are impossible to categorize. There is his application for re-admittance to the "more or less mythical organization" devoted to beekeeping from which he has been expelled. Taylor's gambit: the bees need his help; he can teach them a thing or two about choreography. (In Taylor's Land of Oz, this seems entirely plausible.) But bees are only the beginning of Taylor's menagerie; he writes of devotion to other pets—a bird, a pig, and most especially his dogs. Always, however, these pieces, which masquerade as modest domestic observations, reveal themselves as explorations of more weighty concerns. "My Dear Dogmatist," for example, which begins as a reverie about a pious talking dog, evolves into an essay on love, mortality, and the comforts of atheism ("earthly life is heaven enough").

While Taylor uses many voices in these selections, if he does have a characteristic cover, it is that of curmudgeon. This misanthropic mask is so convincing that when a condensed version of "Two Bozos" appeared in the *New York Times Magazine*, an outraged reader wrote to the editor that Taylor seemed "insensitive to the 'little' people."* (One of the "bozos" responded, defending the choreographer as gracious and pointing out that Taylor was pulling the reader's leg when he suggested otherwise.†)

But no matter how cantankerous he tries to be, ultimately Taylor can't help himself. He's a sweet and generous guy, even if he doesn't want the word to get around. In fact, Taylor is such a straight shooter that he is unable to take aim at anyone—even critics ("Poggie in the Quiet")—without also turning the gun on himself. In the end, no matter who comes under fire in these pages, the joke is always on him. And if there is anyone who enjoys a good joke, it is Paul Taylor.

*Al Devito, Letter to the Editor, *New York Times*, November 15, 1992.
†Hef Daniel, Letter to the Editor, *New York Times*, December 13, 1992.

*f*ACTS

WHY I MAKE DANCES

No one has ever asked me why I make dances. But when flummoxed by the financial difficulties of keeping a dance company afloat, I sometimes ask it of myself. Dance makers are most often quizzed this way: which comes first, the dance or the music? This conundrum was answered most tellingly by the celebrated choreographer George Balanchine, who said: "The money." Nobel Prize winner Orhan Pamuk has often been asked why he writes. The savvy answer in his *My Father's Suitcase*, that he writes to make himself happy, was so meaningful and struck such a chord of recognition in me – his devotion, his steadfastness, his anger – that it caused me to ponder my own reasons. Motivated by Balanchine's sensible quip and Pamuk's candid perceptiveness, this is how I might reply:

To put it simply, I make dances because I can't help it. Working on dances has become a way of life, an addiction that at times resembles a fatal disease. Even so, I've no intention of kicking the habit. I make dances because I believe in the power of contemporary dance, its immediacy, its potency, its universality. I make dances because that's what I've spent many years teaching myself to do, and it's become what I'm best at. When the dances are good nothing else brings me as much satisfaction. When they aren't I've had the luxury, in the past at least, of being allowed to create others.

From childhood on, I've been a reticent guy who spends a lot of time alone. I make dances in an effort to communicate to people. A visual medium can be more effective than words. I make dances because I don't always trust my own words or, for that matter, those of quite a few others I've known. I make dances because working with my dancers and other cohorts allows me to spend time with trustworthy people I'm very fond of and who seldom give me trouble. Also because I'm not suited to do the jobs that regular folks do. There is no other way I could make a living, especially not at work that involves dealing face-to-face with the public. I make dances because crowds are kept at a safe distance. That's what proscenium stages are good for.

Dance-making appeals to me because, although group projects and democratic systems are okay if they work, when on the job I find that a benevolent dictatorship is best. I don't make dances for the masses, I make them for myself. That is, even though they are meant to be seen in public (otherwise, what's the point?), I make dances I think I'd like to see.

I'm not above filching steps from other dance-makers, but only from the best—ones such as Martha Graham and Antony Tudor—and only when I think I can make an improvement.

Although there are only two or three dances in me— ones based on simple images imprinted at childhood—I've gone to great lengths to have each repeat of them seem different. Because of the various disguises my dances wear, viewers sometimes mistake them for those made by other choreographers. My reaction to this depends on how talented I think that person is. Imitating a chameleon has always come easy. Maybe it's genetic, or a protective artifice. The only identity that bugs me is that of the lauded personage. This is because the responsibilities demanded by fame are nuisances that I could easily do without. Ideally, my work would be anonymous.

Stylized lies (novelistic truths) for the stage are what the medium demands. I love tinkering with natural gesture and pedestrian movement to make them read from a distance and be recognizable as a revealing language that we all have in common. Of particular interest is the amorous coupling of men and women, as well as the other variations on this subject. In short, the remarkable range of our human condition.

Whenever a dance of mine is controversial it brings me much satisfaction. One of my aims is to present questions rather than answers. My passion for dance does not prevent me from being terrified to start each new piece, but I value these fears for the extra energy they bring. Getting to know the music I use is a great pleasure even though toilsome. After making sure that the rights to use it are affordable, each piece needs to be scanned, counted out, and memorized. Since I've not learned to read scores, this can take an awful long time.

I make dances because it briefly frees me from coping with the real world, because it's possible to build a whole new universe with steps, because I want people to know about themselves, and even because it's a thrilling relief to see how fast each of my risk-taking dancers can recover after a pratfall.

I make dances, not to arrange decorative pictures for current dancers to perform, but to build a firm structure that can withstand future changes of cast. Quite possibly I make dances to be useful or to get rid of a chronic itch or to feel less alone. I make them for a bunch of reasons—multiple motives rooted in the driving passion that infected me when I first discovered dance. The novelist Albert Camus said it best:

> A man's work is nothing but this slow trek to rediscover through the detours of art those two or three great and simple images in whose presence his heart first opened.

AN EARLY INTERVIEW

Hello, this is Bethpage Bulova-Trit calling for the *San Bernardino Gazette*. Is this Paul Tylor?

Uh, yes, I think so. Only it's Taylor, not Tylor.

Might you speak a little louder, please. Your voice sounds awfully distant. Am I disturbing you?

Uh, no, not at all. I was expecting something sometime.

It is now exactly five o'clock. My publication arranged this interview last week with your press representative. You knew about this, did you not?

Mmmmm.

Hello, hello, are you there? It is exactly five and I am Bethpage Bulova-Trit calling from San Bernardino. My periodical is featuring an article on modern dance.

Oh, now I get it. This is five o'clock.

Yes indeed, it is exactly five in the morning. Is this the noted choreographer to whom I am speaking?

So it's five on the nose, right? And Friday morning already.

Pardon me but this is Wednesday. Would you prefer me to call back later?

Yes. I mean no. It's fine. I'm awake now.

Then I may proceed with my questions?

Shoot.

First of all, what is your view of the latest trends in the world of creative dance; secondly, what is your evaluation of the golf carts our city manufactures; and thirdly, how do you feel about your company performing here?

No kidding, is it? That's nice. I hear it's really exciting to be in San Luis Obispo. Lots of earthquakes and stuff.

Indeed it is. However, this is San Bernardino. Have you not heard that we have far more earthquakes than in San Luis Obispo?

I heard they can be pretty damaging all over the place.

Oh my yes! It is quite thrilling. You should see how our chandeliers and porcelain quiver. Why sometimes even the typewriters walk themselves right off the desks. I myself write with a genuinely antique Remington, you know. The keyboard was designed for the sight-impaired and has all capital letters. But please, Mr. Tylor, I have a number of interesting questions for you and a deadline to meet.

Call me Paul if you want. Your name is Trip, right? Sounds familiar. I think maybe we've talked before.

How extraordinary of you to remember! Except I am now Mrs. Bulova-Trit, not Trip. I once attended a master class taught by you in 1963 at the Manifest Destiny Day School, where I was enrolled as a girl.

Oh, sure, now I remember. But weren't you a boy in the cast of a kids' dance recital there?

Yes, that is more or less true. I was cast as a boy in the recital but, when in your class, my cast was a plaster one. You expressed concern and wanted to help. You kept saying, "Bend it, bend that leg! Why won't it flex, you poor little guy?" You do remember that, Mr. Tylor, do you not?

I've always wondered why your leg was so white and so much fatter than the other one. I thought you'd be limping for life. Does it bend now?

Yes, thank you. May we return to my prepared questions?

Right, enough chitchat. Let's get on with it.

My next question concerns your artistic efforts, a subject which could be of interest to many of our readers. Please describe your Creative Process in detail.

My what?

Your Creative Process, the particular method you employ when forming dances.

Oh that. Well, my creative progress . . .

No no, not your creative progress, your creative *PROCESS*. If you like, we can get to the progress part in a moment, but first to the Creative Process.

Oh, that. Well, what about it?

Precisely to which system of choreographic creativity do you subscribe?

You want me to say how I make up dances?

Please do. I shall quote your each and every word.

Sorry, but I can't say anything about that. They don't let me.

Well, for heaven's sake, why not? Who does not let you?

The choreographers' union. It's very strict about that kind of thing. There'd be a lot of plagiarism if us dance makers went around telling everybody how we make up our dances.

I see.

Ask something else. I bet you'd like to know what I eat for breakfast.

Oh, all right. What are you having?

Nothing. I never eat breakfast. What time is it now?

It is exactly four minutes and twenty seconds after five. What will you be having for luncheon?

I don't eat that either.

Dinner?

No time for dinner. I go to bed early.

And what time would that be?

I don't know exactly. Us dance makers refuse to be clock-watchers no matter what the union says.

But then how long do you sleep?

Well, let's see—counting naps, plus the time it takes to be fully alert, and adding both things together, I'd say the total time is usually about as long as I'm actually lying flat-out.

I see. Do you dream much?

And how! That's when I do my best work.

You mean to say that your Creative Process occurs in your sleep?

No, not my creative process, my digestive process.

Forgive me, but did you not say that you refrain from taking meals?

I said breakfast, lunch, and dinner, nothing about snacks. Maybe you'd like to hear about my digestion. I'm kinda proud of it.

Ah, so you have an unusual digestive system?

You said it! Sorry if this sounds like bragging, but I'm practically the world's eighth wonder. My stomach has been written up in several medical journals, and *The Guinness Book of World Records* is even after me. Just now, in fact, I thought it was them calling.

Really? Just what is it that makes your stomach so special?

It's like this: I used to have a huge beer belly, but now it's the flattest thing you ever saw. It's so flat nobody can figure out how it digests anything.

My goodness, that is an unusually flat stomach. What happened to your old one?

First off, half of it ate itself up, see? And then the other half scrunched down into practically nothing.

No! Not really?

Yep. I used to need suspenders to hold my pants up but now I'm back to belts.

Marvelous! No more out-of-style braces.

Right. And nobody can snap them anymore either. Plus

my fly is reachable. But maybe you'd better forget I said that last thing.

Yes, mentioning your fly does seem a bit personal. However, my readers will need to know if you sleep with anyone.

Come again?

Do you sleep with someone in the nude?

I sleep in my pajamas under a blanket, sometimes two, only the top one sometimes slides off.

Come now, are you not begging the question?

Okay, if you must know, I usually have a lot of cracker crumbs in bed with me. But let's keep that under wraps. Haw haw, what a good pun!

Indeed, I shall not tell. Be assured that it will be our little secret. Well now, I believe that covers everything.

Covers everything- that's a good one too! Thanks for calling, Mr. Trip. It's been swell talking with you. Keep on bending that leg.

Thank you, thank YOU, Mr. Tylor. Should I have any further questions, might I phone again? Hello? Hello?

* * *

A letter to Don York, who wrote the music for seven of my dances and for many years was the Company's orchestra conductor.

4 Apr 94

Dear Don –

Here's the telephone interview you asked for. I can't imagine it being set to music, but if you decide to go through with it, you may want to have a mezzo-soprano do the woman's part. Whatever, I was thinking she should sing loud, wavery, and way up high, just out of her range. Jenny Tipton would probably be able to light her so that everybody can see lots of spray shooting out of her mouth and a big Adam's apple that bobs up and down. As a type, she could be sort of a cross between Florence Foster Jenkins and Adolphe Menjou. My part could be done by a whisky-basso. Not Eartha Kitt, more like the movie star Aldo Ray. I liked him very much. You remember him? He did the sergeants, he was big, lovable, clumsy, slow on the trigger, and had the kind of voice you could barely hear. For visual interest we might give him a slippery telephone to drop, one with a cord long enough to get good and tangled up in. The woman's telephone might be a cordless one in the shape of a large sea shell or ear trumpet.

The more I think about this interview as a libretto, the more I think all the words should be replaced with la la las and scubie dos. Anyway, just remember you asked for it.

Love,
Paul

LETTERS TO SUSIE

Susanne Shackelford, née Butts, is the daughter of R.B. Butts, who farmed and ran a summer camp for boys in Bethesda, Maryland. When I was nine years old, I went to live with the Butts family and eventually Susanne and I became longtime correspondents. Three letters to my dear friend follow.

THE REDHEADED SPIRITUALIST

27 July, 93
Long Island

Dear Susie –

Hi, it's me again. Or, as the formidable Victorian lady explorer always called out when approaching cannibal villages, "Halloa, it is only I!"

From what you say in your last letter, your boss at the library doesn't quite grasp the value of what your ghosting activities may be accomplishing. Maybe someone should tell her that you deserve a raise, seeing as your overtime efforts to bring public attention to Mrs. Robey's ghost may be turning the library into a big tourist attraction—Purcellville Horror. You know, just like the Amityville Horror. Road signs into town can say, "Danger ahead, watch out for falling rocks and Mrs. Robey." Amityville, incidentally, is not all that far from here where people pay good money to visit its spook house.

Now I'll tell *YOU* a ghost story. As in tit for tat. It's a true one, or as close to the truth as my resistance to varnishing memories will allow. At this time (Elusive Retirement temporarily forces me to settle for a short vacation), I've become too attached to my hammock to do any serious work, such as thumbing through "The Turn of the Screw" or reading up on witchcraft or whatever I'd have to do to write a convincing ghost story. But am sure you could in a flash, what with your Gift, no matter what your boss says about you being too imaginative. The following has to do with the man who sold me my Long Island place, his "cleansing" of it, and—this part is sure to grab you—your *DAD*! Yep, the very person who, if the unvarnished truth be known, I still—even in my advanced maturity—fondly think of as being my adopted father:

About five years ago the previous owner of my place knocked at the door. We had met briefly twenty years before and had not been in contact since. Victor "Zak" Zakaine is his name, a metal sculptor, poet, health food proponent, herbal physician given to occasional stabs at acupuncture, advisor to the lovelorn (when answering poetic missiles), obliging astrologer, volunteer tarot reader, and goodness knows what else. When we first met, after sizing me up with a penetrating glance, he greeted me with the kindest of words and warmest of welcomes—from a curious position down on the floor, legs folded haphazardly and hinting of free-form yoga. I also detected a leaning towards the simple life, seeing as the house had no furniture. What was clearly the man's trump card, his most endearing trait, was his ever-buoyant enthusiasm.

A real-estate agent had been reluctant to show me the house. He said that every time he brought in a buyer, Zak wouldn't sell. But I had insisted on seeing it. The property turned out to be better than anything I had ever dreamed of, or probably could afford. A hermit's haven—Robinson Crusoe beach, jungly greenery, sunsets, solitude. (My edges seriously frayed, I needed a quiet place to mend.) When I asked Zak what he wanted for it he replied that, before telling me, he would first need to do my astrological chart, and asked me my exact time of birth—a statistic I'd never thought useful enough to learn. Playing along, I made something up. After spending quite a while figuring out the astrological chart, then comparing it with an even more complex numerological one, he told me the price of the house would be eighty-five thousand, a ridiculously low figure that he based on information gleaned from the charts. (The sham time of birth haunts my conscience to this day.)

He had been looking for a buyer who would care for the house as much as he did, and just to make sure, one whose charts matched his own. Zak truly loved this house, even though its natural setting seemed to make him uncomfortable—the cawing of crows, the flitting of bats, stinging insects, sleep-wrecking songbirds at dawn. He did not feel at one with them. The poison ivy made him particularly uncomfortable. And, like the timid souls who attended your graveyard lark, I suspected that, when star-gazing at night, he would not have been caught dead without a flashlight. Zak appreciated nature theoretically. Ecology yes, the outdoors no.

During the fifteen years that had passed between our first meeting and when he came back to visit, he had not changed a bit. He still looked exactly, almost unnaturally, the same. Same penetrating glance, same bright red hair (I still questioned it), same type of clothes (were the laceless Nikes dated or ahead of their time?), same smooth wrinkle-free face, so smooth that he may as well have had no features at all. The only change was a pretty eight-year-old daughter in tow. She was wearing a spotless white dress, coyly fluffing it with great pride. I couldn't help suspecting her of being the kind of squeaky clean kid that I wish would fall into a mud puddle. Zak informed me that while in California he had been learning to be a shaman.

(Dear Susie, my darlin' "sister" of good times done gone, yet never lost, I'm doing the best I can to make a long story short. You wouldn't want your dad's big entrance not to have a proper buildup, would you? The preceding stuff about Zak is absolutely necessary.)

Hoping Zak would not be put off by certain changes I'd made—plantings of flowering weeds and grasses native to the area; a field of goldenrod; thickets of elderly bladder-wort sympathetically nursed along; a carefully tended tub of poison ivy; impassable barriers of cat briar, etc. —I offered to show him around.

Within a cool dark grove of Norway spruce he was quick to notice a circle of thirteen "chairs"—sections of logs I had placed around an old overgrown Boy Scout hearth. The arrangement was intended to resemble a fairy ring or poor man's Stonehenge. A blaze of fireweed grew out of the hearth. According to local lore there is an Indian burial ground somewhere nearby. In the '20s Boy Scouts camped in the grove and rooted around for arrow heads, tomahawks, fire water bottles, and such.

Zak asked me if I had seen or sensed any "presences" in the grove. Nope, I was afraid not, as I wasn't too sensitive in that way. But surely I'd seen or sensed something strange about the house? Well now you mention it, every so often the bedroom won't let me sleep.

His question prompted me to say whatever I thought he'd like to hear. Not wishing to disappoint him, I added. "Something happens at midnight, whenever there's a full moon," then for good measure, "Cut flowers droop, my dog bristles then howls hysterically. In fact we both have to move downstairs if we want to get back to sleep."

Zak said he wasn't surprised. The "manifestation" was only to be expected. According to him, the room was suffering from "seizures of friction."

"You mean the room is unstable?—probably just an architectural flaw," I remarked, before remembering how proud he is of designing and having had the house built strong enough to withstand the worst of hurricanes.

"Noooo, not that," he answered mildly, then went on to confide the source of the friction:

"One bright night—a full moon was making me rather nervous, not to mention horny—I got home around midnight. Relieved at being out of the moonlight, I went upstairs to the bedroom only to walk in on my wife, who was with a motorcyclist she'd picked up somewhere. She proposed that he move in with us. I did not want him to move in with us. One thing led to another, built into a screaming match, and my wife and the cyclist went off together. Eventually I got a divorce. From what you tell me, the room is still reverberating from that horrible night."

After selling his house to me, Zak had moved to the West Coast to start a new life. He took the biggest and best of his huge metal sculptures, several tons of anvils and blowtorches, his two giant dogs, and, last but not least, a new sweetheart. All snug in an overstuffed truck, they started off to California.

However, as they were coming around a curve in the narrow driveway, I was biking up it. (I had no car, having spent my last cent on the house.) We bumped. Simultaneously apologetic, we both backed up. Simultaneously we both went forward, then backed up again. These polite maneuvers would have gone on indefinitely but for Zak having a flat tire.

Patience, dear Susie Q, your dad will be coming along shortly.

After I helped change the tire, Zak, his smooth face barely crinkled by a radiant smile (indeed, his whole body seemed to be made of radiance), said, "Oh, by the way, you'll be needing a car to tootle around in. As a housewarming gift, I want you to have my old one. You will find it in the garage along with the keys and ownership transfer."

The house had been left in apple-pie order. Windows washed, floors waxed, basement emptied. For my convenience a long list of recommended stores and local residents had been thumbtacked inside a closet door—stylish, a real stylish gent. Was there no end to Zak's considerate generosity?

Evidently not: fifteen years later, at the time of his return visit, he had said not to worry about the bedroom's bad vibes, that he would cleanse it for me. To tell the truth, my waking up in the night has more to do with visits to the bathroom than ghostly vibrations, but I'd been reluctant to say so.

He had needed something wooden to click together for a "cleansing ritual." "Oh, Daddy, not again," his little girl had sighed. I offered two popsicle sticks but they wouldn't click right so we settled for a wooden salad fork and spoon. Instructing me not to talk to him until he was done, he went off down the path to the beach to begin his ritual, leaving me stuck with the daughter, who, by eating popsicles without sticks, was upset over soiling her white dress.

On his return I heard tap tap tap coming up the path, then click click click around the house. Two more times around the house, then whack whack whack up the stairs and into the bedroom. It was taking quite a while and the daughter, bored and restless, was making the stains worse by scrubbing at them with handfuls of bladderwort. Giving up in desperation, she then began to amuse herself by prancing around in some poison ivy.

At last the clicking stopped, and Zak came down saying that it was now all right for me to talk to him. He seemed dazed, as if emerging from a trance. "All clean?" I asked condescendingly. "Stupid rituals. I'm hungry, when do we eat?" mumbled the little girl.

Zak said that the room was now sleepable. Furthermore, that he had been able exorcise the whole property. He had met an American Indian on the path back from the beach. They had conversed. The Indian had been left behind by his tribe from Connecticut, and, according to Zak, was seven feet tall, with skin more white than red, dark hair and eyes, and slightly buck teeth.

"Was he wearing a breechcloth and war bonnet?" I asked.

"No, just ordinary farm clothes with big black rubber boots. Smelled gamey, sort of cowish."

Voila, Susie! What big farmer taught me to milk? Now doesn't this ring a bell?

Zak and the Indian had made a pact. The Indian would cease guarding the Indian grave and escort the dead to their happy hunting grounds. If not for Zak's obvious sincerity, my response to all this would have been a Bronx cheer.

Instead, I mentioned something about the Indian belief of not owning property, merely inhabiting it, and said that I should not have minded if the guard had wanted to hang around. Then, thanking Zak as best I could for the thoughtful, if somewhat colorful, favor he had done me, I waved him and his daughter off as they drove down the driveway.

There was no flat this time, only an eerie repetition of our simultaneous maneuvering. As I waved and started back towards the door, Zak also reversed and backed up. He had forgotten to ask me something—had there ever been anyone in my life who fit the guardian's description? This time I didn't need to humor him or even think twice. Your dad, of course, my guardian and role model during my happy farm days with him.

Later on that evening the phone rang. It was Zak again, telling me that, after reviewing what I had said about Indian Rights, he had been able to recontact the guardian. Everything had worked out splendidly.

"Gee, that's swell," I said. "You mean he is staying?"

"No."

"Well why not?"

"Because the tie is cut."

"The tie? What tie?"

"Your tie with the Indian, of course. He is the doppelgänger of an idealized father figure of yours. But you have outgrown the need for a guardian or mentor. An immature notion of needing guidance was holding you back. Now you are free."

All I could think of to say was a polite "Oh, I see."

Zak's message seemed to be a mixed blessing, like receiving a warm hug and a corrective slap on the wrist at the same time—both heartening and mortifying. But that Zak's astrological delvings could have revealed that my secret and long-nurtured idealization of your father was unacceptable. It made better sense to simply chalk it up to down-to-earth insights on Zak's part. Either way, his intent was touching.

Switching over to his soothsayer mode, he went on to predict that my near future would bring fabulous gains, of which I was delighted to hear but had my usual doubts about. (Gains? A gain of weight? Me being overweight, a gain would be to lose some.) I envied Zak for his belief that life is essentially good, and appreciated his obvious effort to transfer optimistic expectations, yet an opposing side of my nature ruled out such expectations.

After we hung up I thought: Oh, brother, good old Zak, his enthusiasms are wonderful, so kind, so . . .

The phone rang again. Now what? What else could he possibly see in his crystal ball?

"Hello again, Zak."

"This is not Zak, this is the MacArthur Foundation calling. Is this Mr. Taylor?

"Speaking."

"Congratulations, you are being awarded one of our unconditional five-year grants."

That was when I dropped the phone.

So much for things that go bump in the night, phone in-cluded. If you think your dad would like to read this, it's okay by me. Please tell him that I don't believe for a minute that my tie to him is cut, and that I still can't help thinking of him as a role model.

So long for now. Maybe you and yours will come treat me to a real visitation one of these days. I'd like that a lot.

Big fonds,
Yr. old big "brudder"

A PERPLEXING SITUATION

Aug, 93

Dear Susie,

Now about me sitting on the Queen of England's hand, since you ask. And I thought nobody ever would. Well, it was at the Shaftsbury Theatre in '91. Or maybe '81? Anyway . . . oh, now I remember—I didn't sit on her hand. I meant to say she sat on MY hand. Sorry, but can I help it if memory tends to brighten up the past?

The Queen, heavier than she looked, had come to see my company perform at the Shaftsbury Theatre in London. I'd been instructed very carefully on the protocol expected of me—Yes, Ma'am, no, Ma'am, and such—by the Queen's Emily Post. I forget his exact title, the guy in charge of good manners. He had a fruity-looking garter on, walked funny, and told me that when the orchestra started playing "God Save the King" (it's like our "Oh Beautiful for Spacious

Skies and Amber Gripes of Wrath"), I was to follow the
Queen down the center aisle, then let her step aside so that
I could pass ahead of her into the front row of seats. This
was because I was supposed to end up sitting on her right.
"She's to get out of my way and I'm not to sit on her left,
right?" I asked, just to make sure I got it. "No, not on her
left, right by her right, in the seat adjacent to her RIGHT.
The Queen's lady-in-waiting is to be sitting at the Queen's
left. Now then, Mr. ... um ... Mr. Taylor, have I explained
the seating clearly enough?" He'd begun to look concerned
so I said "Don't worry about a thing. I gotcha. Thanks
Ma'am, I mean Sir."

The part about stepping in front of the Queen seemed
sort of off but not worth making waves about. Since I wasn't
getting my own lady-in-waiting, at least the Queen wouldn't
have to make way twice. Actually, I kind of liked the idea
of going first. Pecking order is still a big deal in Britain, and
the London audience would get to see their Queen following a Virginian of French descent to his seat.

But the protocol guy hadn't mentioned anything about
what type of seats to expect. They turned out to be the
tricky pop-up kind that won't stay down by themselves. So
when Ma'am got to hers and was about to sit, I reached over
with both hands and pressed her seat down for her, only I
didn't get my left hand—am pretty sure it was my left—out
in time. Wow, let me tell you, when those queens sit they
really mean it!

I didn't know what to do; what was the protocol for

that? Given the situation, you can understand why its solution didn't come in a flash. This is what went through my mind: If I leave my hand there, maybe she won't notice? But she's apt to sit there till intermission, which could be in two hours, depending on which intermission and how fast the music is played. My poor hand. The elderly conductor is the over-conscientious type who tends to take his own time. But maybe my hand will go to sleep, get numb. Maybe Ma'am won't care for the dancing and get up to leave. Everybody knows she likes horses better than dancers, saddles better than theater seats. Some preference!

In the end (a pun there somewhere), I finally decided to get my hand back. It took a heck of a yank (another!). Ma'am never said anything to me about it. She is a nice queen.

I've since wondered how often she notices or has to put up with someone's hand being there. I like to think that for a moment or two I came close to being a power behind the throne, so to speak. On the other hand—who cares which one?—I can't remember ever being so uncomfortably trapped and royally put upon.

Lotsa love,
Paul

BOAT TRIP

1 Jan, 96
Long Island

Dear Susie-

Hope and trust your Christmas was a jolly one. Muchas gracias for the thoughtful xmas card with note. Happy to know camera is not only acceptable but useful, once you get the missing film. Sorry about that—I assumed camera came complete with necessary accoutrements. The card that I sent, since you ask, was one left over from about two or so years ago, the year I misplaced my address book. Rather than starting a new one, which I'd probably lose again, I decided against sending new Christmas cards this year.

Are you ready to hear about my wonderful week-long cruise? Well, here goes, ready or not: the interesting Christmas dinner served aboard the boat, a square-rigged barkentine with one of its four masts doubling as a tall skinny smoke stack, was slow to appear, and then when it did, was mostly burnt. This was understandable, however, seeing as the cook and three of his helpers had jumped ship, the kitchen being taken over at the last minute by several good-sported if inexperienced crew members from the deck. To be precise, they were from the starboard side of the quarter deck. (Where the heck that was was for them to know and me to find out. By the end of the cruise I still didn't know, but had learned to locate my own cabin almost every time!) The blackened food, however, was not bad, was even tasty, in a way, but some of the passengers—not the greenish ones who had already hastened to their cabins—sniffed a bit about the china having dark thumb prints and the salad dressing tasting of tar.

The Captain, Jurgen Müller, splendid in his white uniform with gold epaulets, had been an officer of the German Navy during World War II. There was something cheerfully foxy or secretive about his eyes, but that may have been only the reflections from his grasses or maybe because there were so many women aboard and his wife was back in Germany. Whatever, he graciously filled up the long spans of time between courses by reading to us from his favorite Conrad sea novel, first in German and then in French. I for one might have enjoyed it more if he had read Patrick O'Brian in English. Anyway he meant well and was doing the best he could under the circumstances. That the lights went out didn't help any. Something was wrong with our generator due to the ship's rocking motion, which caused the water in the swimming pool to overflow, splash down a companionway and get the generator all wet. But our Captain was not able to finish the reading because, just as the lights came back on, an ominous ripping sound came from somewhere directly above. This was soon followed by tramping noises and a shrill whistle. (No, it was NOT your ocarina—we may or may not get to that later.) A crew member rushed in and announced that the main jib had split. Captain Mueler politely excused himself, explaining that he thought he better go investigate. That the sail had split seemed strange because the breeze was light and the boat's rocking gentle.

For dessert we were served a fancy kind of frozen tart "mit sloggen," meaning whipped cream (my German was increasing by leaps and bounds), also poufaroles or something like that, of which I ate several left by those passengers who didn't feel quite up to them and had left to be queasy in private or to hang over the ship's railings. Some people get seasick and some people don't; I was one of the lucky ones. Besides the desserts, and the fruits and cheeses after them, there was a lot of wine left over and so I was able to have one of the waiters slip me a couple of bottles for later. He looked just like a Santa's helper but turned out to be an unusually short Turk. There were all sorts of nationalities represented by passengers and crew—mostly German and American but also French, Australian, English, Swedish, Russian, Caribbean. But only one Turk, and a small one at that.

Oh, about the cabins: Naturally, since the ship is a commercial enterprise and its owners interested in cramming in as many passengers as possible, the cabins were spatially economic, not roomy at all. Really quite cozy, in fact. I met a lady, Karen somebody from Perth Amboy, who was sharing a cabin with her brother, or so she said. When unpacking his ditty bag (more nautical talk!) he had gotten jammed between a post and the port hole so that they had to call the cabin boy to come help pry him loose. In all fairness to the ship's owners I should add that he, Huey, the so-called brother, was not exactly underweight. Nor was their cabin boy, come to think of it. (I never saw my own cabin boy, only the goodnight candy he left on my pillow.) Karen also told me that she had become fond of a certain tropical concoction offered at the ship's

bar, namely sex-on-the-beach. "I have sex-on-the-beach for only five dollars," she boasted. She was always good for a laugh and we often conversed at the bar early in the morning. I went there to smoke (after being reprimanded a few times for fooling around with my cabin's smoke detector) and she went there because her "brother" not only took up more than his half of the bed but was a big snorer.

Then there was the attractive if prim English girl who, when being helped by an admiring sailor to step from the ship into one of the small black shore-going inflated rubber tenders (tenders are tended by tender tenders), managed to disengage her breast from his friendly clutches and fall overboard or, as we say, into the drink. Well, the members of our crew didn't get too much shore leave, so you can understand how they had to take advantage of whatever opportunity presented itself. The girl's name was Mary, or possibly Celene, and she was traveling by herself, preferred to be alone, and was not easy for me to chat with. I suspect the word had gotten around that I was writing a scandalous article on the passengers. This was not at all the case, but was perhaps related to me telling the management that I'd been hired by a magazine to write a travel article and, since nicotine always makes reporters think better, I needed to smoke while writing it. Admittedly, this was not quite accurate. I only said it in hopes of being allowed to smoke in my cabin.

My favorite passenger was Mary, who was from the outskirts of London somewhere. The reason I liked her so much was because of her being so inspirational. That is, she was 92, refused to stay home in her rocker, instead made the most of the time left to her by traveling all over the world with her cane and her 85-year-old companion. She even went for swims at beaches and let the surf roll her around. Several times I had to pull her out, getting my cigarette pack wet in the process. She and her companion didn't seem to get along too well, particularly at "tea" time, otherwise known as the ship's happy hour. She could swear like a sailor, but that didn't make her any less inspirational. In fact, quite the opposite.

My other favorite passenger wasn't actually a passenger. He was one of the engineers and had the most magnificent handlebar mustache I've ever run across. He took me on a tour of the engine room, explained the whole complicated arrangement in detail, and didn't seem to notice that I didn't understand one word. Even better, he was the best, or at least the most individu- alistic, dancer aboard. He was a bobber, a perpetual motion machine, bouncing up and down every night  to international cocktail music played on a vibraphone by the ship's music man (Polish) and scooting his various danc- ing partners around as if they were shopping carts. He was round and white like a tennis ball, spoke mainly Spanish, or possibly a mix of Spanish and Finnish. The ladies he got to dance with him were usually thin and always at least a foot taller. Later in the night he would get extremely happy and continue bobbing without a partner. Steadying himself by gripping a rope or the capstan or whatever was handy, he increased the tempo of his curious cork-like motions while twisting the long up-curved ends of his mustache and adding joyous flourishes with his free arm. In the mornings—we often breakfasted together—he drank rum with a raw egg in it and seemed hardly hungover at all. Though his dancing was impressive, what I liked best, envied him for, was his view of the world: He loved everybody—everybody except politicians and policemen. Ship captains, he said, glancing sideways, were "okay," which I interpreted as a tactful way of saying they weren't.

Well, I could go on and on describing the entertaining people I ran into but maybe you'd rather hear about the itinerary. The boat, I mean the square-rigged whatchamacallit, left from Barbados, then sailed to Tobago (much hawking of beads in Tobago), then Grenada, off of which the afore-mentioned jib split, then slowly on to Curaçao, where the same thing hap-pened to several  other sails, which caused the sail-sewers to murmur and shake their heads and forced my friend the engineer to spend most of his time down below with his engine.

By motorized screw (pardon the bad word but that's

how we call the propeller) we then somehow missed Bequia (who needed another Spice Island anyway?), then put-put-putted on to St. Vincent, or possibly it was St. Barts, where I was sorry not to behold the giant fringed Basilisk but did capture the common brown Roach and several unusually slow and tattered tropical Buckeyes with my colander in the restricted area of a rain forest when nobody was looking.

Some other islands followed, but by this time I was more intent on seeking the giant fringed Basilisk than memorizing islands' names or even what day of the week it was.

On some island or other we were herded by a loquacious guide up the side of a 3000 ft. volcano, where we had the rare treat of inhaling smoke from the sulfur vents. Delightful. Someone should bottle it. Our guide, a local, was a card. Pretending to be a Carib Indian priest luring a sacrificial virgin into the largest vent, he gently tugged on one of the prettier women in our group, saying "Cummon, honey, les taka walk." This was on St. Lucia, now I think of it, where I've been before, only on the other side. There are two volcanoes, twin peaks. Just one of them works.

Suddenly we were back in Barbados, where one of the two biological lecturers, the ecologically correct one enamored of lizards, the one who, though frowning upon insect collecting, shockingly sported lizard skin belts, informed me that there was no giant fringed Basilisk in the whole Caribbean, never was and never would be, but that if there was, those "hardhearted unecological natives" would have eaten them all up. Oh, well, that's life.

Any New Year's resolutions this year? Are they the same as last year's procrastinations? Or was that the year before? I looked for your list but have temporarily misplaced it. I only have one resolution and that's to have fun, more and more fun, even if they have to throw me in jail for it.

It's snowing again and Car-Car refuses to manage the driveway. Guess my dog, Budd, and I will have to miss rehearsals for another day or two, relax and enjoy being snug and warm by the fire.

Wishing you and yours perfect health, super joy and the very best new year ever

Yr. wayward big bro,
Love, Paul

*AUREOLE**

At this time—'62—modern dance is still keeping its distance from lyricism, "pure" or unexpressionistic kinds of dance, and reassuringly melodic music. There are a few exceptions—José Limón and Pearl Lang have done pieces that are primarily movement structures meant to match their Bach scores. But most modern choreographers are still oriented to asymmetrical angularities and use music such as Bartok or Wallingford Riegger—modern, but not too modern. *Aureole* has been commissioned by the American Dance Festival, where anything old is out. Unable to resist quirkiness, and always eager to ignore trends, I've accepted Handel, hoping to rankle anyone at the festival who thinks modern dance has to limit itself to modern music or weighty meanings. Am also

---

* *Aureole* (1962) was my first big success. A lyrical, pure-dance piece, set to the music of Handel, it was created for the American Dance Festival, which generally featured the more Expressionist work of José Limón and Martha Graham.

hoping that a change of diet will be good for both audience and myself.

In another way, the dance is an attempt to get what I've learned in Louis Horst's classes out of my system. As Louis would've wanted, the dance's steps have been limited to a few basic seed steps—themes to vary in speed, direction, sequential order, and any other way that might make them seem less redundant. My favorite step in *Aureole*—a certain run with flyaway arms—is a direct and intentional steal from Martha's *Canticles for Innocent Comedians*. It may be a little off, but it's the closest I could come.

Something about the simplicity has been on my mind. No puzzlements for folks to ponder, no stiff-necked pretensions from classic ballet, or even any of its steps. It's just old-fashioned lyricism and white costumes. By the way, Dr. Tacet, who's designed and sewn the costumes, isn't happy about having to use elastic from Jockey shorts for the girls' waistbands, or about me substituting a white bathing suit for tights. And he pouted some when I ripped his ruffles and suppository-shaped decorations from the girls' skirts and tossed them into a trash can.

The dance's many entrances and exits are an attempt to give an illusion of a larger cast than five and to open up the stage space so that the dance will seem to be happening in a larger one than is bounded by the proscenium. The best parts of *Aureole*, to be seen only backstage, are the dancers' hurtling races through the dark crossover in order to make their next entrances on the opposite side of the stage. There are likely to be graceless collisions with unwary stagehands, the dancers' onstage expressions changing into ones of something less than angelic serenity.

As far as choreographic invention goes, and virtuosity, there isn't much of that in my duet with Liz, but at this time there isn't a high premium put on these things. Even in this "pure" piece, feelings are foremost. Dance is a meaty word, and, naturally, there's more to it than firework displays. The duet is built on my own feelings for Liz—part fantasy and part real. As she changes from a comely kid with scrawny shoulder blades into a radiant woman, my admiration is on the upswing. I intend the duet to be easy and warm, also formal and distant. It's hard to say if the formal part is fantasy and the easy part is real, or vice versa. Liz and I never discuss it, but the duet is a reflection of a real relationship, one that, as usual, is loaded with inexplicable duplicities.

The solo for me isn't set until the rest of *Aureole* is finished. This is due to procrastination pure and simple. I've told myself that the other dancers must first be well rehearsed and secure in their parts. But now rehearsal time is running out, and the long solo, which I'm beginning to wish in the worst way wasn't so long, is set on the commuter train to Adelphi, where I sometimes teach. In order not to attract attention, I stay in my seat drawing little stick figures in a pad and later copy the anatomically possible ones with my body. It's like learning a dance by mail—deciphering one of those Arthur Murray Teaches Dancing in a Hurry footprint diagrams. The main difficulty lies in keeping the flow going by passing through, rather than hesitating in, each position. It's been irksome to see other dancers lock themselves into positions as if to say, "Get this, everybody, I'm perfect—think I'll hold this pretty pose a while longer in case your slow eyes don't notice." Though I'm able to get the hang of it, the matter of flow, as well as other things particular to the way I move, may become a problem if the role is ever taught to someone else.

The solo, done almost entirely on the left foot, is also unusual in that it's an adagio. Usually, in classic ballet anyway, adagios are danced by women. Though I haven't intended to get too involved with meaning, the Handel has a hymn-like sound, and, to amuse myself more than for any other reason, I've made the part as if it's to be performed by some kind of earth father who goes around blessing things. Doesn't travel much, but indicates expanding space with développés of arms and legs toward the four cardinal points. If done in a gestural way, these slow-motion semaphores may give the effect of being in an open plain which extends beyond the theater and out into the stratosphere. I have myself a pretty big image—Father Nature, religion, and the cosmos. The balances are deceptively difficult, but the solo's hardest part is the entrance in silence. It's a simple walk from the wings to stage center which has to be unselfconscious, friendly, and seem inevitably right. No matter how often I've practiced it, this easy walk scares me to death. It's going to strip me of dance steps to hide behind and leave me stark naked.

When *Aureole*'s premiere is only a few days off, four of its sections have been set, but not the fifth and final one. By my bending Horstian rules, the seed steps have become unreasonably transmuted beyond recognition. They're twisted backwards, sideways, and inside out. I've hit the bottom of the barrel and can't think of one more blessed way to vary them for the finale. How to fill up the remaining music? I tell myself what I once learned from Bob Rauschenberg—that the easy way is best—and go over to the rehearsal tape machine to snip off the last pesky movement.

Just then the noted dance writer Edwin Denby comes into the studio to see a run-through. He often treks to nickel-and-dime performances and ratty studios, where, if asked, he offers hesitant and gentle criticism. It's late morning and he's probably been up all night writing poems in a microscopic hand, then left them to walk his thin frame and long feet from West Twenty-first to Thirty-eighth street, perhaps savoring some noteworthy examples of ironwork facades along the way. Another guess is that he's arrived with no change in his pockets, he being the city's softest touch. Also generous with his time to many unestablished dance makers like myself.

Dancer Bet offers Edwin some coffee and shoos the studio cat from the middle of the floor. Tabby's always getting underfoot and loves to bask in beauty in the golden rectangle of light that falls from the skylight. Tail twitching, the cat saunters off in dignified retreat, then veers around to take a picturesque pose on Edwin's lap.

After we show the dance, Tabby seems unimpressed, but Edwin blinks cheerfully.

"Well, what do you think?" I ask, deep down preferring a couple of choice compliments, not criticism.

He answers mildly. "I think that perhaps it could be even better if a little something is added to finish it off."

"But, Edwin, there's no time! And ending this way gives more importance to the duet. It makes an unexpected ending."

This is wishful thinking. I know he is right.

Wishing us luck on the premiere, he apologetically nudges Tabby off his lap, rises, then shyly backs out the door.

With little time to lose, the dancers and I tackle a concluding apotheosis or coda. Unable to bear the dull prospect of more tinkering with the same old used-up steps, I throw together the first that come to mind. A bunch of dizzy tilts, turns, breakneck cavorting. Even if the dance is no good, at least we'll have a workout.

And then on a bright day in August, Bet packs our costumes and magnetic orchestra into one small case and we all train up to New London. During the trip she completes a pair of tights she's been knitting for me, needles clicking away like Madame Defarge's. Dark-eyed Sharon is looking nicely complementary sitting next to Renee's fair splendor. Liz is radiating enthusiasm, and Dan prattling. I'm a million miles away and scanning fields for butterflies—whites and sulphurs to match the fluttering ones in my stomach.

Arriving at Connecticut College, seat of modern ferment, ivied asylum of creative sweat, we go backstage to hug our lighter, Tommy Skelton. He smiles and bobs his Adam's apple up and down for us, looking a lot less skeptical of me than he has in this same place ten years ago. It's a homecoming. Merce and his troupe are the resident company this summer, along with José and his. I trust that Tommy's student stage crew will be more adept than I was. They're beginning to look awful young. Larry Richardson, who's pulling curtain, will one day, like me, be taking to the road with a group of his own. Here we are, all one big family. Am supposing that I can put up with a little generational repetitiousness.

The gang and I are to share a program with Katherine Litz, a dancer of delight whose solos are delicate flights of whimsy, a phantasmagoria dreamed up by an eternal ingénue. She does dilapidated aristocrats, fragile souls at their toilets in the twilight, romantic matrons with girlish tremors. My favorite is a dithering enigma in a sack. She never ceases to cheer her audiences, never seems to mind that her work isn't widely recognized, and never mentions her solitary struggles to continue work that deserves higher acclaim. We, her friends and fans, are nuts about her, but sometimes there are a few in the audience who seem confused by Katy's ladies. Let's face it, these are insensitive jerks. No art and no genius can ever be without touches of haziness and mystery. It's a big honor to be sharing the same program with her.

At the dress rehearsal in the darkened Palmer Auditorium a large piece of plywood has been placed across the back of some center seats. On it is Tommy's usual clutter of cue sheets, shaded desk lamp, metal ashtray brimming with Gauloise butts, and something new—a flashlight. Also as usual, Tommy's headset has gone stone deaf, and so technology is being replaced by primal shouting. "Put another amber gel on the special that's over stage center," Tommy calls to the crew.

Preoccupied with a sense of impending doom, I've finished a long warm-up and, curious to see what Tommy has up his sleeve in the way of lights for *Aureole*, jump down off the apron and grope up the aisle. Noticing the flashlight, I ask nervously, "Does that mean you're expecting the light board to blow?"

"Nar," he twangs. "Your solo's gonna be lit dark. It's for you so's you can see your way around the stage when you're dancing. I'll have a giant spotlight follow Dan."

"Skeleton, I'd have thought by now you'd have gotten rid of your New England twang. Hey, what's that ugly rope dangling down over there stage left? And what's that wrinkle in the cyc? And why does this proscenium look so slanted?"

"Don't worry. Everything will be fixed by tonight. We'll

have the audience all lean to one side so the proscenium will look straight."

Tommy's wit knew no bounds. Right now, though, I'm thinking he's not so funny. "Dancers, come out onstage so we can see what your costumes look like under light," I call, wondering how everyone can be so cheerful when we're about to dance the worst mess since spaghetti.

Tommy says, "Paul, how do you like this sunshine effect? Pretty gorgeous, huh?"

"Everybody looks yellow. If I'd wanted Orientals, I'd have gotten some in the first place."

"But that's the color of sunlight. We mix green light with lavender and out comes sunlight, see?"

"Yeah. I see green and lavender edges on their faces. Can't we just have plain white people in plain white light? Let's dump the sunshine this time. Also that soft focus you use for ripe old stars. Who needs it anyway?"

In professional lighting circles, uncolored light is considered poor taste. Tommy, like his teacher, Jean Rosenthal, favors shaded depth over flat visibility and has learned to mix his palette not like a painter's but according to unfathomable laws of light. However, more out of friendship than out of artistic beliefs—compromise being another word for friendship—he humors me by yanking all the gels.

After the dress rehearsal, I go downstairs to a dressing room where I make up to fateful ticks of my watch, indulging in as much fear and insecurity as I want. Involuntarily, my left big toe is twitching a little dance of its own. Can't help wondering if that might be a sign of approaching insanity. I get up to put on a dry dance belt, put it on upside down, take it off, put it on wrong again, sit down, get up, sit down. (Recollections need to be somewhat choreographed.) Noisy watch tells me to get into costume. I skid into Bet's room next door and say in a totally expressionless voice, "My costume. I can't find my costume."

With a double gesture, one hand denoting pity, the other disdain, Bet replies, "Oh, *Paul*—you have it on!"

How stupid of her to be so clever. Dutch Treat was always saying annoying things. Miss Treat is her other name. And she peppers her food, too. Heavily.

What happened, and how *Aureole* felt to perform, are things that are nearly impossible for me to describe. To pare it down to basics: The curtain lifts, we depart from this world, find a far more vivid place, and then the curtain closes.

Toweling off quickly, reveling in relief at being not too tired to still walk, the dancers and I grope for each other's hands and force our leaden feet to scamper back onstage for a speedy bow before the audience gets a chance to escape. I'm making an effort to look humble when a tidal wave crashes into us. They liked it; we like them—in that order. Catching a sideways glimpse of Sharon, I notice her brown eye brimming.

Friends and faculty come backstage to say complimentary things. Pal Babe's hand appears from between two people, offering me his program. On it are written the numbers of bows for each dance. By *Aureole* is a circled "12." Across the cover is lettered "I like Katy best." The Babe, bless him—tact was never his strong suit.

Wonderful Merce Cunningham drops by to say he's thought my dancers wonderful, and grand José is gracious and supportive. Other than the experience of dancing itself, these rewards are best.

None of the troupe has any idea that this has been the first performance of a piece that we'll be dancing hundreds and hundreds of times. On five continents, in world capitals and Podunk towns, in North African desert heat, at the edge of Alaskan glaciers, in the moonlit Pantheon's shadow, under banyan trees. With happy hearts and grapefruit ankles we're to dance it in Rotterdam, Rosario, Riga, Rio, and Istanbul—in more corners of the globe than you can shake a leotard at. *Aureole* is to be performed in big, fancy opera houses and on shaky postage-stamp platforms, on slick parquet and splintery planks, on wax and linoleum, and broken glass. It's to be danced with amoebic dysentery, Montezuma's revenge, bleeding hearts, and yellow jaundice, with sprained backs, split soles, torn ligaments, popped patellas, and a hernia or two. The usual. Orchestras of all ilks will play astounding tempi, often the correct ones. Magnetic tapes waver and sputter out, but the dance persists. We're to get quite tired, yet Handel never falters. He's our novocaine.

There are to be garlands of jasmine, too, often looped around our necks by almond-eyed strangers. At times paupers or great fortresslike socialites come to say that they've been touched in some meaningful way. Kings, queens, and bag ladies are to see it.

Today it is strange to imagine the many *Aureole*s that are danced by other companies, casts in many places, mostly dancers I've never met whose limbs move through the same shapes as ours, and who've probably grown similar calluses. God bless their poor little bare toes.

After the premiere, critics express surprise at the American Dance Festival for including a "white ballet" on its programs and write that *Aureole* typifies just about everything that modern dance has been trying to do away with. Allen Hughes of the *New York Times* says that it's "different, daring, and delightful."

"Delightful." I was to argue with the *Times*? Yet there's something… If I could only duplicate myself and send one of me out front to see what it looks like.

Later on, when out with an injury, I was able to see it, and my nagging doubts were confirmed. The dance had been good to me. I appreciated it, valued and trusted it, but was out of sympathy. Though I understood its audience appeal, for me it had little. I too enjoyed seeing dances that required little effort to understand, ones that gave uplift and caused a smile. Yet I was not smiling. I couldn't forget how relatively easy the dance had been to make and how previous dances, both larger- and smaller-scaled, had stretched my goals much further. *Aureole* had been child's play compared with others that I had to dig for, grapple with, and slave over, ones that had a more developed craft to them but weren't as popular. It was impossible to know if it would continue to be appreciated; yet for all its success, perhaps because of it, *Aureole* filled me with resentment. I was wary of it. It caused me to see a time coming when a choice would have to be made—to remain on the comfortably safe side of the doorway to success, or to pass through it and into a tougher and lot less familiar place.

— From *Private Domain*

MARTHA CLOSE UP

She's come to New London for a brief visit, and I first catch sight of her as she crosses the huge lawn in the center of the campus. A small dot in the distance, she's dressed in red and is carrying her own lighting equipment—a red parasol that filters the bright day, casting down a flattering shade of pink. I change direction to get a better look. Closer up, what has seemed like a smooth regal glide turns out to be a sort of lurching swagger. Her face features a crimsoned mouth artfully enlarged, and she's wearing sunglasses. Behind them the eyes—the eyes!—the eyes are dark and deep-lidded, and there's something very wise and undomesticated in them, like the eyes of an oracle or an orangutan. That is, they look like they've seen everything that's to be seen in this world. Maybe even more. They give the impression of being placid yet at the same time seem to be spinning around like pinwheels. After the mouth and the eyes there's this more or less unimportant nose. And as seen from up close, her grooming is telling me that everything possible has been done to prevent nature from taking its course. Just as our paths are about to cross, she stops, dips her chin down, and looks up at me. I've never heard Martha Graham described as cute; nevertheless, that's how she looks as she waits for me to say something. I become confused. Other than throwing myself at her feet, what would be acceptable? Forgetting to disguise my southern accent, I say that all us students sure are thrilled that she's finally come. (Theatrically speaking, her two-day-late entrance has been an effective buildup.) Lowering her huge lashes, she whispers that being there is, for her, like atoning for all past sins. Immediately I'm dying to know exactly what all her past sins have been, but it seems best not to ask. There have been rumors that she isn't above laying out a student or two, and that she once kicked Anthony Tudor in the shins for accusing her of choreographic compromise. Apocryphal or not, these incidents only add spice to her ongoing legend.

Facing a legend is a blast, but making me jittery. The mouth is uttering oracular things—something about the "little flags of celebration which fluttah all over one's bodaah" (deepest tone on the "bodaah"), and about the "miraculous little bones of the foot," and she's seeming practically gaga. Then she's telling me she believes I can be a very great dancer if my imagination holds. (Does she mean that it would take imagination to think of myself as great or what?) She's also saying that I'm one of only two people whom she's ever said this to. (Who's the other? I'll kill him.) Then she produces a slip of fortune-cookie-sized paper and writes down the phone number of her school, saying that she wants me to join her company before the year is out, and that when I get to New York I should call.

Her exit is preceded by an authentic-looking Oriental bow, with flowery wrist gesture thrown in for good measure. I stand transfixed as she diminishes into a floating red dot against the wide green lawn. The lurching swagger had been pretty nice, and saying bodaah a big improvement over instrument, but what I'd loved best were the oracular eyes.

— From *Private Domain*

CLYTEMNESTRA*

The overture is starting and the curtain's soon to levitate. Other dancers and I are waiting in the wings, some chatting nervously, others trying to get in the mood to, as it says in the program, rape Troy. Tiny Martha is standing alone upstage center on a blue-carpeted ramp, looking very calm. In fact, her stillness might be taken for complacency, even boredom. But it's not. She's a monumental mote, a doughty dot, an electron at the quiet center of a spinning atom. Her hairdo is towering higher than usual, and her giant eyelashes have been heavily beaded with wax. Protruding from under her brocaded skirt is a big toe which, either from so many years spent dancing or from being crammed into too many small shoes, or both,

* Martha Graham's most ambitious dance work, *Clytemnestra*, premiered in 1958 at the Adelphi Theater in New York. The commissioned score was by Halim El-Dabh, the décor by Isamu Noguchi. The cast included Graham in the title role, Bertram Ross, Helen McGehee, Ethel Winter, Yuriko, and me.

has grown in an unnatural direction, crowding neighboring toes, and now slanting sharply inward. Eyes cast down in Buddha-like contemplation, her face is as durable as a porcelain mask, one that is to express Clytemnestra's story of treachery, murder, disgrace, and final rebirth. Her concentration breaks for a moment, and she turns her head to the wings to hush us with a queenly hiss.

I've probably mentioned that my feelings for her aren't simple? Love, awe, fascination are spliced to a dimmer view, and, once in a while, stresses tug at my commitment to her. Yet, right now, seeing her stand so monumentally, so alone, I feel nothing but admiration for this small, feisty woman who, for at least thirty-two years, has been lifting dance to new heights. Besides, her knowing eyes have seen something wonderful in me, and I'm determined to be worthy.

Two curtains lift, one after the other (overpaid stagehands finally get the order right). An interesting but not quite Mycenean throne sits downstage right. There are two singers, one at each side of the apron. A third curtain—a row of vertical golden bands—rises, and Martha stands revealed. The audience scrambles to their feet and welcomes her warmly.

Drowned out by this ovation, Halim El Dabh's music becomes inaudible. Considerable delay before Martha's first move. When the commotion quiets, she begins a series of repeated clenched hand gestures and in-place treadings, almost matching herself to the corresponding thonks in the music. When the music goes on to something else, however, she soon goes right along with it, doing only one or two thonks too many before regaining her bearings.

Precision in a lesser dancer is not nearly as great as Martha's inaccuracies. Personally, I like her mismatching of steps to music, for then the steps don't seem so obviously phrased. I also enjoy seeing her choreograph her body into snarls and then find such wonderful ways to get out of them.

But right now I'm putting my mind on the rape of Troy. It's the only part of the dance when I'll need to be in unison with the other guys, and it's quite a challenge. Something about the way I move—shades of timing, force of attack, not sure what—makes me stick out in a group, and even though I've worked hard at it, fitting myself in has been a problem. Maybe it's because my approach or mental outlook isn't the same. Being an ex-swimmer, I remember how nice it feels to press against water. I can't resist using air in the same way. Counterbalancing the imaginary weight of space makes my body feel that it's accomplishing something. Though I've tried many times to dance with less pressure and weight, that always feels weak, willowy, and extremely stingy. Martha's probably just about given up on me being in unison, and to tell the truth, I don't really mind. But tonight I'm determined to do my best to rape Troy exactly like all the other guys.

They dance great—Bert Ross, David Wood, Gene Mc-Donald, even the others who only get to clutch spears, tote dead bodies off, and such. Except for David, all of us are six feet or over; all move forcefully and archaically; all conform to the concept of a flat two-dimensional figure that seems to be Martha's idea of a man. Naturally, her dances stem from her own point of view. We're usually stiff foils, or something large and naked for women to climb up on. A few of us would like to be more 3-D and think that less beefcake would be a good idea, but have been scared to say so.

The girls—Ethel Winter, Helen McGehee, Matt Turney, Yuriko, and the newer ones, such as resplendent Ellen Siegel—are all terrific, too. Helen, usually cast in ingénue roles, is wonderfully wiry and vengeful as Electra; Yuriko, movingly dramatic as Iphigenia; Ethel, glorious as Helen of Troy; Matt, always a favorite with audiences and company members alike, makes a gracefully broken and appealing Cassandra (unison dancing isn't her strongest point either, so she's easy for me to identify with).

All of us have been thoroughly trained at Martha's school in a methodically developed vocabulary. We are seasoned performers with strong techniques and understand Martha's choreographic aims clearly. None of us is all that young; the majority have had college educations. Most of the men started their training later than the women, in our early twenties.

What happens for two hours after *Clytemnestra*'s opening curtain is to be described, photographed, analyzed in depth, and stored in libraries for future reference. There seems to be little left for me to add, except a few unrecorded, and probably unimportant, impressions. Most have to do with feelings and sensations difficult to describe, ones that, even if described, may seem unlikely, yet they're true, or as true as remembered feelings can be.

Inside, at a million m.p.h. or more, corpuscles are zipping around and filling me with a sensation of great speed. Otherwise, I'm experiencing a feeling of superslow ooziness. This of course has little to do with actual rates of speed but is because of something that, for lack of a better term, I'll call the dancer's clock. Focus or concentration makes the time different for when you dance and when you don't. No ordinary timepiece, like a drug, this clock stretches stage seconds, implanting eons in between—also compresses performing years into an outrageously short span. So I'm both speeding and oozing at once, scooting through space, slithering through time, eating it up and savoring each swallow. A flick of the foot and I'm airborne.

Bright stage light is coming from all angles clinically, like under a microscope or on a vast, borderless desert. I'm basking there. Adding to the hot light, internal rays are traveling out through each of my pores.

Besides the music, such sounds as street traffic, murmuring from the wings and burbling from the plumbing are magnified to a high pitch. Lint on a drape, the flavor of sweat, the odor of a stagehand's ground-out cigar are noticeably present. Hearing, sight, taste, touch, scent have become paranormal. Present is also a sixth sense—let's call it will power. I can will myself into midair, hang there forever. By means of another, even more mysterious power, I'm able to control what the audience sees, can direct their eyes to any particular part of my body—my left shoulder, my right elbow, both bunions at the same time. Anywhere. When a dancer is hungry, determined, or motivated enough, almost anything is possible.

Steps are Aegisthus's voice. Lunges bellow, spins scream, skitterings whisper insidiously. From someplace down low a carefully controlled spasm ripples up through the torso, arm, and finally out through the tip of a recently acquired limb—Aegisthus's black leather whip. It's as if he's saying, "Look, everybody. Slime! Fury! Sadism! Dementia!" There is no doubt in my mind that I've been given a franchise on wickedness.

Great greedy gulps from an empty Noguchi wine cup. Rapturous reelings, slow darts. While in the midst of a cartwheel, I study the details of an upside-down proscenium. Hedonistic burning sensation of soles whisking across boards. Softness of a leap's superslow spongy landing. Softness of blue-carpeted ramp against rump. Softness of featherweight Martha in my arms.

For her safety, I shift into low gear, support her gently, treat her as spun glass. According to the whorls of my fingertips, her silky smooth veil feels roughly corrugated.

Wantonly, we plot the murder of Agamemnon and the usurpation of his throne.

Aegisthus motions: "There is the dagger. Take it."

Queen motions: "Oh no, I could not possibly."

Aegisthus motions: "Sure you can. Just let me help you to place your hand on it. It's over here in a pocket of the throne somewhere. Somewhere here…Rats! The stupid prop man's forgotten to preset it. No, here it is after all. Grab on, O Queen."

Queen motions: "Mercy, it does feel nice. I do like daggers."

Aegisthus motions: "Wait a minute. Your dress has gotten caught up on something. May I be of assistance? There. Now you can go do your dagger dance."

Leaving me to sit on the throne with the purple veil in my lap, she begins a long, demanding solo. Since I'm downstage in bright light, it might be easy to draw attention away from her, but this wouldn't be cricket.

I've figured out that I'm here because she needs a strong presence onstage, a kind of energy bounce to help keep her from lagging, to be a presence for her to battle. I should keep alive for her, stay in character, yet do nothing distracting. I've placed a safety pin to mark a place in the veil that I'll be needing to hold in order to manipulate it right. Keeping my face down so it's in its shadow, I slowly, unobtrusively inchworm the cloth through my fingers, maintaining the tension until, safety pin found, her solo completed, I fling the veil over both of us and spin her off.

When the curtain goes up on Act III, Clytemnestra and I are draped over her bed. She's having a bad dream, then leaves to go dance with others. I'm going to be on the bed for thirty minutes or so, so I've tried to get myself as comfortable a position as possible, which isn't simple, the bed being not exactly a bed but one of Noguchi's stony and treacherously tilted abstractions.

I'm "sleeping" the best I can when suddenly, from out of the blue, Martha returns and starts pummeling my stomach. I'm thinking that maybe she's come up with better things to do than the planned ones—something that the older dancers have warned me about. (Ad-libbing at premieres is not unknown. Later on, things get more precise.) I flick her fists away, then roll over and go back to sleep. She likes it when you play along with her.

She soon comes back to pummel me some more, and I keep flicking her fists away, rolling over, and trying to keep myself from falling off the bed. After a while she leaves me alone and goes off to dance with Bert, Helen, and Gene.

After the final curtain, on her way to the dressing room, she says, "Pablo, I noticed what you were doing on the bed. Naughty! Let's keep it in."

Clytemnestra is a resounding success. Both public and press immediately accept it as a masterpiece. Among many other tributes, Martha is praised for her merciless integrity and for being a colossal figure in a theater of her own intellectually preconceived goals. John Martin of the *Times* writes that "the girl still holds promise." A more heartening and sincere tribute could scarcely be paid to her.

Her company is also extolled, and I'm singled out for praise. My part of our duet is deemed a deep characterization. This is very gratifying, since my role, though an important one, isn't as large as I would have liked and could have been lost in the shuffle.

The last performance over, I pack the theater gear, return to wet sneakers, cold loft, Tabby's mouse patrol, occasional disagreements with Tacet. Within a batch of bills is an eviction notice from the Housing Authority, accusing me of illegal living. I relegate it to the trash basket and hide the hot plate.

— From *Private Domain*

A man who lives where SoHo and the Village meet writes:

One night last week, I heard the most awful sound. It was my old friend George yelling from the street. Maybe he was being murdered. I tore down to the front door and found him pointing at a man who was trying to break into my car. I said, "Hey, that's my car. Get away." The man didn't move. I said, "Look, there's nothing in there you want, so go on." It was as if he didn't hear me. I said, "That's my car. What are you doing!"

He said, "I'm breaking into it."

I told him I was going to call the police, and went back to my apartment and tried to get 911, but I kept being disconnected. I went downstairs again, and the man was lounging on the fender. Then another man showed up, with a pair of pliers, and the two of them started fooling around with the car door. I said, "What do you think you're doing, anyway?"

The second man said, "You leave him alone."

So I said, "Are you nuts? That's my car you're fooling around with."

Then he accused me of being crazy myself and said, "Well, if that's your car what's the license number?" I wasn't going to tell this clown anything, so I said, "What's your number?" He wouldn't tell me, either. So I said that now I really was going to call the cops. But I still couldn't get through, so I went back and found that my pal George and the two men had all disappeared. I began to worry that the men had kidnapped George. Then the phone rang. I ran back to my house, and it was my friend Sophie—as usual, wanting to know how I am. I mentioned that George seemed to be missing, but I didn't tell her about the car burglars— that would have taken too much time. (She often doesn't listen, and you have to repeat everything.) After I got Sophie off the phone, I went out to look for George. The two men were there again, operating on my car with their pliers, and no George anywhere. I'd run out of things to do, so I said, "Now I'm really mad. You don't go away till I get back." I went inside to look for something to drive them away with. The fire poker was just the thing. I took it outside and held it up for them to see. It was only fair to warn them.

One of the men clapped his hands to the sides of his face and said, "Oh, I am so sorry"—a surprise, because I didn't think I was looking all that menacing. He pointed down the block to a car exactly like mine. "That's my car," he said. "No wonder my key wouldn't fit."

"Yes," I said. "That's how you tell when it isn't your car."

"I'm sorry," he said again.

"Oh, that's all right, forget it," I said.

They went and got in their own car, and I went back to the house. Just as I remembered about George, he showed up. He had gone to get some milk. I told him that everything was O.K., that the men had mistaken my car for theirs. But George said he still didn't trust them, because my car had a baggage rack and the other one didn't. We went out to see what the men were up to now. They were at the movie house down the street, hauling out furniture and loading it into the car. That was something I couldn't get much interested in. I mean, they weren't moving furtively, or anything. But I did wonder why, if George had noticed a car like mine down the block, he hadn't said anything. It would have saved everybody a lot of brouhaha.

—From *The New Yorker*'s "The Talk of the Town"

TWO BOZOS SEEN THROUGH GLASS: AN EPIPHANY

A quote from the poet Paul Laurence Dunbar, "It is important that we never know why the caged bird sings," is now at the top of my pet budgie's bird cage. Many of the words are hidden by a passion flower that day by day winds itself into an elaborate snarl, leaving less to read and more to puzzle about. Unfamiliar with the quote's context, I keep wondering exactly what the words mean, trying to read between the vines, so to speak.

While balancing on a wobbly telephone book, I had painstakingly squeaked out the quote with one of those nearly dried-up magic markers. That was a risky thing to do for the sake of something I admired yet did not quite understand. I could have broken my neck!

Sometimes, usually when I am daunted by the responsibilities that go along with being the head of a modern dance company, the words seem to imply something about a search for contentment, implying that if we knew why the caged bird sings we might want to go live in a cage too. Not a bad idea, if you ask me; think of all of us in our own private cells, balancing adroitly on cute little swing perches and chirping contentedly. What a happy world. Safe from each other, too.

At other times, when blue or infected by maudlin nostalgia, it seems to mean that the caged bird's song is not actually a song but the sound of sobbing done in a musical way. Was a pitch being made for artistic expressionism? Or were Americans being sad about governmental censorship at the National Endowment? Maybe President Bush's family values and lack of leadership on AIDS matters were implied. Or is it only something to do with music being a palliative?

Like a painting, like a dance, like any type of art, the quote forms a vehicle to take a ride in. As I have come to understand it, most artists construct mysterious containers, the contents materializing or becoming clear when blended with our own personal memories and past experience. What we are able to see or hear is what we get.

But then there are times when one does not care to play the interpretation game, and there are rainy days when Bird (my budgie's name) does not sing. Rain is what activates my pet pig, Sugar, a four-hundred-pound Yorkshire White who is just wild about mud puddles.

Following a dry and chilly spring, it has been raining a

lot out here on Long Island's North Fork. Yesterday, while attempting to connect two old hoses, an odd feeling of inadequacy came over me, self-doubt having not quite displaced the cocksureness of my youth. I assumed that the feeling was only because of the hoses' tangles and beat-up threads but should have known that the whole operation was pointless, that it would rain the minute I turned on the sprinklers. Well, the next time it rains I will know what not to do.

But back to art. Intended as a helpful guide, the following story, a sort of autobiographical fable, may clarify and even explain how Bird's cage fits into the picture:

Once upon a rainy day, just when fat old gas-bag Sugar had backed herself into a mud puddle and was blissfully pumping some awful smells into her cute little bird bath, two dancers who study at my company's school arrived.

I had asked them to learn an old solo of mine in the city and then show it to me out here in the country. If I liked what I saw, one of them would have my permission to perform it at Lincoln Center. Without assistance from me they had taught the dance to themselves by deciphering some runic notes and watching a brittle film held together with Scotch tape. I had not been particularly interested in having the dance revived but the sponsor had offered a generous fee. The two dancers had now come to audition. Because of the time it takes to bus here they were to spend the night at my house—an unusual but necessary interruption to my highly prized solitude.

The one whose name kept escaping me explained that he was Carl Flink. Both the name and the bearer seemed kind of clunky. Eyes widening, he then asked "You keep a pig? *YOU* keep a pig?" A sudden bolt of embarrassment hit me, a feeling that I had let this star-struck dancer down. "Look here, son," I answered, "what did you expect—a couple of rhinestone-collared wolfhounds? Just because a person is well known doesn't mean he can't keep a normal ordinary everyday pig." My young fan had misinterpreted me.

After asking if they had eaten dinner and learning that they had but wouldn't mind another, I explained to Carl that clean sheets had just been put on the guest-room bed, making it necessary for him to sleep in the basement with Sugar, who, by the way, has a persistent itch that she alleviates by rubbing herself against anyone who happens to be around. The other dancer, Hef Daniel, would sleep in Saint Santo's—set and costume designer Santo Loquasto's quarter-scale reproduction of a Southern Gothic Church left over from the PBS TV version of my "Speaking In Tongues." It now crowns the brink of a nearby bluff. Inside are interesting graffiti (easily interpreted), and a bare mattress.

The next morning, when asked if he and Sugar had slept well, Carl said, "Yes indeedy, Boss, it was just like being back home in Minnesota." Hef, or Hefalunk, as I had begun to call him, had changed from his city getup into his country one and was as scantily clad as a lone survivor on a tropical isle, but seemed a bit chilly.

Before breakfast everyone became eager—Sugar bursting to blow more bubbles, my young visitors anxious to make an impressive showing. Dying to get my solitude back, I suggested we save time by skipping breakfast.

Outside on the deck was the best place to show the dance. Hef brought me a chair. It seemed presumptuous of him to think I might have trouble standing up, but I thanked him anyway and mentioned that his strong young legs were not likely to stay that way forever.

Seated inside and steeled against what might be coming, I watched the bozos through a sliding glass door which blurred and made them seem strangely distant. It had begun to drizzle again. They looked uncomfortably damp but squeaky clean, sturdily built, well proportioned, and about the same height (at least I was taller). Like a brace of matched pistols they stood side by side, expectantly waiting for me to say which should blast off first.

While I fiddled with a stopwatch the drizzle turned to rain. Seemingly unperturbed, the two improvised a little shuffling dance in an attempt to scoot rain water off the deck. Realizing the futility of it, they then stood quietly gazing past the church toward cloud-shrouded Connecticut. I sensed that the salty Sound below the bluff had the same magnetism for them that it does for me, and that their fascination with the glamour of dance was similar to what mine once was before discovering that having a name, being tagged and labeled, is a cage not gilded.

Riverlets streamed down the glass door. Through it I was seeing myself doubled. Out of control, my mind shot me back to my youth.

Like many a young tyro, inner voices had directed me to hitchhike to New York City, seek signs of intelligent life, make a name for myself by becoming a dancer, and overwhelm the world. Somewhere along the way, mostly because of a gnawing dissatisfaction with the choreography of my betters, I began to make up my own dances.

One of the first was *Epic*, which was set to the recorded voice of a lady giving the correct time. This was the opening section of *7 New Dances*, a full-evening work that three good sports and I performed at the 92nd Street YM-YWHA's Kaufmann Concert Hall in 1957. Within a small circle of dance-goers it brought not fame but instant alienation, the hall being all but emptied within the first five minutes. Somehow the telephone lady and I had managed to make *Epic* seem a lot longer than it actually was, in fact longer than any epic should ever be.

Too involved with remembering my steps to let the rapid exodus distract me, I never lost concentration or for a moment doubted my abilities. I was heroically single-minded, dangerously idealistic, and, if I do say so myself, enviably double-jointed. But I was still fairly green and had not learned that, contrary to popular belief, at certain times there is little point in the show having to go on.

"Okay," I said to Hef, "let's get this over with. You may

as well go first." Reconsidering, I then added, "To save time, both you two Bozos should do this thing in unison."

As the telephone lady began her spiel the two seemed to become someone else. Their necks took on a soldierly alertness, their ears erected, their whole bodies sensitized, and in their buoyant bearing a heart-tugging bravery. Too assured and too young but maybe all right in a pinch, I thought.

The dance had stemmed from my fascination, practically a mania, with human posture—the everyday shapes our bodies take on, ones so common that they are usually ignored or only unconsciously noticed. It was astonishing that past dance makers had pretty much neglected these magnificent building blocks, and I felt it a duty to frame and point out their appeal. The ordinary shapes of standing, sitting, kneeling, and so forth are nothing less than a universal language, rudimentary perhaps, but they could be nothing less than a Rosetta Stone (alas, "a nightmare alphabet," according to *The Herald Tribune*). Gestures are regional, their meanings changing from country to country, yet from the cradle on we and our brother beasts, birds, and bugs tell each other many true, false, or secret things through posture. Visually speaking, I would say it is our oldest language, one with an extensive vocabulary both primal and penultimate. To nourish and expand the art of dance with ordinary posture was more or less what I intended.

Who is to say what is and what is not a dance? Modern dance guru, critic, and editor-in-chief of the monthly *Dance*

Observer, for one, a man whose own posture, by the way, was not exactly above criticism. He succinctly communicated his stance on my Y concert with four inches of blank space. It is alarming to think how he might have reviewed the Judson choreographers, a group that sprang up in the Village about ten years later and whose work I could not help but view as a ho-hum rehash of the Y concert.

I mean no disrespect when speaking of Louis Horst, now deceased. I had studied under him at Juilliard, where he was one of my favorite teachers. He cared deeply for what in his day was contemporary and contributed generously, devoted a lifetime, to updating dance, yet it was difficult for me to accept views that seemed passé. Perhaps he felt a touch of generational envy, envy similar to that which I felt when seeing two young men through rain-streaked glass.

"Stop!" I yelled. "You've gotten the sequence mixed up. Now you'll have to start over and we haven't got all day. Your bus back gets here at noon. Pick up the tempo, count faster. In fact take it double-time and get those dynamics right! The long stillnesses should look dynamic and the short moves relaxed, not the other way around. Doesn't anyone teach dancers how to hold still these days?" And these guys were likely to become teachers themselves someday, even form dance companies of their own. Good grief, it seemed that modern dance was beginning to be locked into generational redundancy.

Of all the dance roles I have ever made for myself, the

Epic solo was probably the most difficult to pull off. It was hard to keep the still moments from going dead and required intense concentration to remember the sequences of moves. Through repetition in rehearsals dancers' muscles usually remember sequences for them, but because this solo had little continuous flow of movement, and what there was of it was consistently interrupted by pauses of different lengths, the sequence had to be remembered mentally. Instead of the usual relationship between metered movement and music, each move and stillness was assigned a different length of time, which contrasted, rather than followed, the rhythmic pattern of the recorded music (the numbing lullaby of that darn lady who was forever reminding us of passing time). In addition to memorizing the positions, it was necessary to memorize a staggering number of grouped counts, each count lasting exactly one second. Learning the twenty minute-long *Epic* was like trying to memorize a telephone book.

"Okay, guys, let's give it another go. This dance ain't easy but you're doing fine." Recalling how hard the solo was, I was now seeing them differently. "Let's not split hairs. Just remember two things—dancers are superhuman and adequacy is a dirty word. "

When the dance was first performed I had hoped that a strong stage presence would make up for the lack of virtuosic steps. I had already developed a fairly solid dance technique and assumed, perhaps wrongly, that I had earned the right to throw that type of skill out the window. However,

I still needed to learn that, as sublime as simplicity may be, it can produce snores.

In the fifties, naturalism, or my version of it, was not in style and in theatrical dance never had been. I owed much of my inspiration to two friends, the painters Robert Rauschenberg and Jasper Johns. They had begun to create, not naturalistic or realistic paintings of things, but certain presentations of the things themselves—Coke bottles, American flags, an unmade bed—objects judiciously selected for their form and imagery, classic clichés that were then recycled into a magical new life. Bob had suggested the business suit worn in *Epic* and Jap, the section that was merely a simple pattern of everyday walking. (The four-minute duet that featured unadulterated stillness was my idea, for which I take full blame, and did.)

Collaboration with these two artists as costume and set designers continued until 1962, at which time it stopped when Bob wanted to strap a cumbersome stuffed lamb onto one of my dancers, the charming Dan Wagoner, who later formed a fine company of his own. By that time I felt I had done about as much as I could with found movement and was reluctant to burden Dan with the lamb. However, later on when Bob strapped a chair to dancer/choreographer Merce Cunningham, my much admired modern dance competitor, I thought it looked quite nice.

By the time Carl and Hef got to the head postures—the final group of positions, ones that were subtle, easy to overdo, and the most difficult to pull off—I was longing for time to stop in order to savor each moment. It is impossible to know how a dance looks when you are dancing it yourself. I had never seen "Epic," never really known for sure if it was of much importance, and had only its 1957 reception to go by. I now saw it as being worthwhile.

And my bozos were terrific! Only the risk of seeming maudlin kept me from rushing out onto the deck to tell them that the strength and nobility of their rendition was breaking my heart. I had seen myself in them, the youth I was when mostly dreamy and green. They had proved that this dance was worth the effort, and I could not imagine that it had ever looked as good.

As a duet in unison, the two men would be performing it at Lincoln Center, maybe even at my company's City Center season in the fall.

The rain had stopped for quite a while. With the dancers gone I had gotten my solitude back. So why was the glass door still bleary? Bird's cage, perhaps that was it. Revisited youth was a budgie caught in the net of time, and the squeak of memory's magic marker had summoned forth grateful, joyful, swing-perchy tears.

Bird is now flying free, at the moment buzz-bombing Sugar, and at the top of the empty cage is a quote from James Joyce's *A Portrait of the Artist as a Young Man*: "Welcome, O life! I go to encounter for the millionth time the reality of experience . . . Old father, old artificer, stand me now and ever in good stead."

THE STRANGE STORY
OF HOW I CHASED
AND CAUGHT THE GUY
WHO BURGLED MY HOUSE

Well, we can get to the strange part later, but first you should know that I've always been the territorial type of a person. Anybody wants to come into my house has to get my permission first, see? I guess I was born that way. Why, even as a toddler I felt possessive of my playpen and the teddy bear, pop gun, and other stuff therein, and if anyone dared mess with them without asking I became a pretty dangerous kid.

So then when I got older, instead of going away, the territorial element in me became even more developed, as now I had not one but two places to guard—the town house in New York City and the country one on Long Island, both of which have no burglar alarms because I prefer to take care of interlopers myself.

By the way, the drive from house to house makes me a bi-areal commuter rather than bicoastal, and the going back and forth takes less than one and one half hours each way when traffic cops don't catch me.

Well anyway, as all us home owners know, houses are like children in that they need constant attention. You have to keep your eyes peeled for the wear and tear. My accident-prone city house has gotten fairly out at the elbows and needs the most attention, but I take better care of the country one because it's by far my favorite. When raccoons claw through the country roof to nest in the crawl space I immediately replace the shingles. A couple of other things that need continual attention are the electrical wiring that hungry mice like to gnaw on, and the well's motor that attracts lightning.

Unlike the narrow view of bricks and cement in the city, the country view is wide and therapeutic. Cares and woe just fade into the background and I become an entirely different person: more relaxed, less judgmental, not at all the guy I am in the city. Country joys include flowering weeds, colorful insects, spectacular dawns and sunsets, and a phone that hardly ever rings. For a territorial person who values his privacy my Robinson Crusoe retreat can't be beat.

For many years nobody ever came into either of my two houses uninvited. There were occasional mice or roaches in both, of course, but they don't count. Live and let live is my attitude toward them. They can walk right in and I say who cares, the hell with it. Yet it goes without saying that a total stranger is an entirely different critter.

Well, one time, after pruning the poison ivy, turning

over the compost heap, cleaning the chimney, and such, I drove back to the city still wearing my country duds and hadn't bathed or shaved. In other words I looked crummy. A set of city clothes was in my suitcase that I parked in the front hall. On the way in I was angry to see that a window had been smashed and the window sill was bloody. Further investigation proved that a mantelpiece clock and several gold doodads from my award room were missing. So I called 911. A lot of other people were calling the same number, but I finally got through. Eventually a cop arrived with a photographer in tow. The cop took notes while the photographer snapped shots of bloody fingerprints in the bathroom. When they were done I saw them to the door. It was ajar. I was sure I'd locked it after letting them in. Evidently, the burglar had been hiding in the house the whole time.

After the police left I found that my suitcase was also missing. Besides the city clothes, it contained my bank card and address book. This was not good.

Then the phone rang. It was a neighborhood lady who said she had retrieved my address book from a nearby trash can. I said I'd be right over to get it. On the way I saw a nicely dressed young man sticking a bank card into the money machine at my bank. I thought, Wouldn't it be funny if he and the burgler were the same person? I stopped to stare at him. He turned and ran.

It was some chase. The blocks zipped by. I was sixty-ish and couldn't believe I could still run that fast. I yelled

"Robber, stop him!" Nobody paid any attention. "Murderer, help!" was of no use either. That's the City for you. We might as well have been running through zombies.

Some five or six blocks later, at Houston and 7th Avenue, the burglar began to slow down. I lost sight of him for a moment as he skidded around the corner, then saw him throw down the bank card, which slid out of sight through the crack of a closed warehouse door.

We ran another block or so and suddenly I found myself hugging him from behind with both arms. He didn't resist, just kind of wilted and gave in. I noticed a row of needle marks on his left forearm.

"What did you do with my stuff, you creep?" I asked, turning him around and giving him a good shake. No answer. "You better give me my stuff back or else!" Nothing; still mum.

I was getting nowhere. What to do now, I wondered, "OK, you asked for it," I said, slapping him hard across the cheek.

By then the zombies had come to life. Looking mildly entertained, they gathered into a gawking group to view the fun.

The slap seemed to have no effect. He said nothing, stepped closer, and gave me a hug. It was almost as if he had enjoyed the slap and was thanking me for it.

Now comes the really strange part of this story: I felt sorry for the guy. It had suddenly occurred to me that he was like a wayward child who hadn't had much attention for many years; in a way he wasn't so very different from my worse-for-wear city house.

Nevertheless, he had broken in and my sympathy played second fiddle to my territoriality.

By then several rubbernecking motorists had pulled up. I shoved the burglar to the nearest car and asked the driver if he would take us to the police station. I wasn't sure that my captive would remain passive, so also asked if we could put him into the trunk. The driver nodded, got out, and opened it. As I was cramming the robber in, a police car rolled up. Uh oh, I thought, I look a lot crummier than this guy and now the cops are going to take me away instead of him.

Only they didn't. Without questioning either of us, they clicked handcuffs onto him. A tug of war then occurred between me and the cops with the robber in the middle. I thought if I could get my guy to tell me what he did with my stuff I would forgive and forget. But the cops won out. They put him into their car and went away.

End of story. So much for my strange loss of territorial imperativeness. When thinking about it, a broader view convinces me that we don't really own anything. Life is short, taxes are high, and our possessions are only on loan to us for a relatively brief time.

Art? It's okay but, let's face it, there are lots of punchier things around. Take what's going on right outside my window, for instance. Here, over Long Island Sound, beneath speedy clouds and an early moon, gulls seem to be soaring for the pure fun of it, and below them on the beach, scattered along the shore, magnificent Ice Age boulders are squatting in reverence. There's not an ugly misshapen thing in sight.

So I'm thinking that the phenomena nature creates make what people manufacture and call art seem like peanuts. High culture, low culture, any old kind—isn't it all pretty much second-best? Creatively speaking, it's as if all of us humans are nothing but third-world Kilroys.

And it seems to me that people who make things—ambitious daydreamers, mostly those like myself who'll do anything rather than put on a tie or work for a living—are answering nature's challenge to imitate its capacity for invention by constructing make-dos that we hope will be called art.

Oh yeah, there's hope, fervent hope. After all, the moon can create certain types of insanity, clouds manufacture disastrous storms, gulls are able to squawk forth serial music and leave big messy masterpieces of white on their roosting rocks. So why not us?

And I suppose, humiliating as it may be, a good deal of the materials we use for our make-dos are borrowed, begged, or stolen. Although certain of these sources that we draw from, or snatch, are usually kept fairly well hushed up, I'll spill the first few that come to mind: other people's art (improved upon, of course), accidental discoveries, grudgingly accepted mistakes, adolescent impressions, cultural leftovers from the past, trendy graffiti from the present. And premonitions, let's not forget those astonishing hunches of what is to come . . . it's a shame they're so often crackpot.

Now if you ask me (and *Vogue* has, and is also paying generously, otherwise I wouldn't have dreamed of revealing all these valuable trade secrets), well, this question of cultural classification and interaction is spinach, and the hell with it. Who cares if it's high art or low, or about the relationship between the two? Possibly the art-mongers do, and the paying public, but not me. All I care about is if cultural things work or not, and if I can get away with how my dances turn out.

Really, honest and true, for those who make things— poems, buildings, moon modules, Kewpie dolls, whatever—the whole world is one big, glorious grab-bag!

— From *Vogue*

*f*ANCIES

FOREWORD TO *PRIVATE DOMAIN*,
BY GEORGE H. TACET, PH.D.*

L et us state at the onset that we have never demanded a cent of remuneration for any of our
many invaluable artistic contributions to the success of Paul Taylor's finest dance creations, which is the pri-
mary reason that he finally consented to allow us, George
H. Tacet, Ph.D., to compose this preamble of Elucidations.
It is commendable that the dear boy always listens to our
advice and is here partly acknowledging his immense debt
to us, if reluctantly.

It is a pity, however, that he stubbornly refused to have
us, George H. Tacet, Ph.D., ghostwrite the entire text of
this, his well-meant attempt to communicate foggy memories of an antipodal life trapped and spun inside the dangerously whirling vortex of American Dance. Should we have

---

* I wrote this as a foreword to my autobiography, *Private Domain*, but it
was deleted in order to not confuse the reader.

written it, readers would find him less dichotomous, more stable, and less dizzy. His tendency to dramatize himself would have been stifled, his unseemly boasting curbed, not to mention an entire deletion of his bald-faced admission to having blackmailed his competitors. One can only be thankful that he chose not to mention the time he sent death threats to all the New York City dance critics. We, George H. Tacet, Ph.D., would have included much more about the elegant award ceremonies, Embassy soirées, and high teas amongst royalty, but we certainly would not have mentioned his shameless pirating of dance steps or the inane practical jokes he inflicts on his dancers. During his plodding ascent to a certain degree of fame, his conduct has not been as flawless as one would expect from a more typical example of the American Dream. Frankly, we suspect that he has hoodwinked his publisher by writing this book merely as an exercise with which he intends to teach himself how to write lucrative pulp fiction.

One wishes the dear boy had taken more pains to describe in detail the roots of his Creative Process, and the strong influence that we, his faithful mentor, have had on them. And where is the placement of his work in relationship to Art and Interdisciplinary Culture? Even the connection between his dance creations and those of the Watusi is neglected. We, for one, would be curious to know from whence comes his Inspirational Psyche. We, for another, yearn to be informed of his exact sexual orientation and political affiliation.

Our dear boy's story commences with his humble beginnings, continues haltingly as he dances up the bumpy
road to fickle fame, then irksomely ceases just as his knack
for stylizing human movement approached its apogee. The
reason, he explains, is that there has been a certain influential person vaguely connected to the success of "Esplanade"
whom tact must rescue and compassion shelter. Are we, his
constant guide and mentor, supposed to be grateful for this
omission? We think not.

At any rate, we can say that his life, quite unlike our own,
has been entirely devoted to his Art, or so he maintains.
It is difficult for us to understand how he has managed to
have such a straight and unswerving course. Where are the
excursions into a fuller and more broadening life? Besides
dance, where is the involvement in the other Arts, ones such
as calligraphy or Japanese paper folding? Although mainly
devoted to phrenology, our own talents have encompassed
such diversities as paleontology, analytic psychology, phrenology, Seychellian basketry, and the refinements of the
Aeolian harp.

It is also distressing that our boy has not been able to
make his motivations clearer. What are his emotional root-
ings? Where is an enlightening description of his Id and its
exact size? Why has he not married and produced offspring?
We ourselves proclaim with quiet force our large and interesting Id. We possess undiminished creative powers and
approximately eighteen offspring, most of whom are known
to us by looks if not by name. We take pride in each of our

five marriages. Surely, if shy Paul had married even once, his creative thrusts would have been that much greater.

Why the publisher has chosen to circulate such marginal meandering is indicative of the present decline in the auto-biographical form. In our day (we ourselves having faced and conquered the embarrassing matter of septuagenarian leakage), the autobiography was a grand genre. Then was the golden time when Artists imparted finer things: credos, philosophies, dioramas that reflected and illuminated. Indeed, and this is said with a humble bow, we have recently completed our own biographical history: eight volumes filled entirely with golden pith! Alas, today's publishers seem uninterested in our masterpiece, pandering as they do to the present plague of bourgeois taste. It is shameful that our monument to aesthetic refinement must wait for the re-ascendency of discriminating publishers and a less illiterate public.

Although our dear boy's strangely inconclusive account of his dancing days may satisfy those who like primitive writing and are able to read between the lines, we heartily recommend a more civilized plunge into our own yet to be published opus.

Interested parties may contact:

George H. Tacet, Ph.D.
9898 Shade Lane
Perth Amboy, New Jersey

REAPPLICATION
TO O.H.E.C.

My good friend and neighbor Chris Kelly resembles a leprechaun in height and feistiness and, like me, is full of beans. He was an entomology major at Cornell, now works a local vineyard, raises bees for fun, and keeps several of his hives on my property. Anything I know about bees is largely due to him. His immediate family also raises bees and started a more or less mythical organization they named OHEC (the H stands for honey). Each member has a high and mighty title. I was accepted into the group and stuck with the lowly title of Grub. For reasons too Byzantine to explain, Chris had me kicked out but then kept urging me to apply for readmittance. But each time I did, he had my application rejected on the grounds of insubordination. Playing along with Chris's game, the following request was my third attempt to get back into OHEC.

18 July, 1994

Greetings, genuflections, and humble salaams to thou,
O worshipful Emirs and Emiresses of OHEC. Please, if I
may be so bold as to ask a favor, might thou be so kind as to
give my sincere condolences to thine wayward son Sweets
Kelly on being recently demoted from Prime Emirkin to
His Flatulence Second Class.

APPLICATION FOR READMITTANCE

I, thine humble servant, having undergone a lengthy and
remorseful period of penitent exile, do contritely submit
the following justifications for reentry into thine greatly
esteemed kingdom. It is with high yet humble hopes that,
unlike my two previous applications, this one will be taken
seriously and that I will be allowed to soon attend thine
Conclave of Kings or, as Sweets irreverently calls it, Col-
lision of Queens. No doubt various subalterns will be able
to check this application's facts before the Conclave occurs,
fastidious processing being necessary to maintain such high
standards as thine. However, O Wondrous Beings, before
gaining your favor by listing my latest contributions to the
nurture and nature of our dear little Apis mellifera—indeed, to the whole apoidean field, all of which is certain to
amaze and delight thou—I wish to enumerate a few of the
awards that have been bestowed on me since my last application, to wit:

An impressive, if rather belated, citation from the Boy Scouts of America, presented to me for untying a square knot on the first try without using my hands (rule book says nothing about slicing with a knife gripped between the teeth).

Sensational write-ups in several medical journals and the resulting entry into *The Guinness Book of Records* for having the world's brightest smile without resorting to blackface.

A solid gold statuette (mailed in an envelope marked DO NOT BEND) for appearing on a Voice of America TV documentary that featured thine humble servant demonstrating the highly coordinated facial gymnastic of simultaneously touching nose with the tip of tongue while keeping eyes crossed.

An obsidian plaque engraved with runes from a coven of devil-worshippers (thirteen reborn evangelicals), presented to me in the dark of the moon for being able to recite the Lord's Prayer backwards.

If citing these accolades seems boastful, O Significant Beings, please forgive my presumptuousness. They are mentioned hesitatingly as mere indications of our nation's recognition of my lesser accomplishments, my true calling being to aid in the cultural improvement of our beloved apoidean friends. Believe thou me, O Adorables, my entire mind, body, and soul have been devotedly committed, one might even say permanently agglutinated, to their betterment and uplift. But I am only too aware of my shortcomings. In other words, I know which side of my bread is honey-buttered. Pray make no mistake, my entire life has been one long upward trudge towards the betterment and cultural refinement of Apis mellifera; specifically speaking, to the tasteful improvement of those primitive little dances they do to communicate with each other, and which, by comparison to the contemporary dancing of Homo sapiens, are woefully out of step.

Harken, O Supreme Rulers, it is with high hopes of being acceptable that I lay before thine feet these fruits of my recent labors:

The truly amazing advancements made by a particularly tangle-footed colony of mine that, after stony patience on my part, has finally been taught to do not only the jitterbug, fox-trot, and hula-hula, but the extremely complicated and aesthetically uplifting boogalooga. In addition, the slower members of another colony of mine have all but mastered a simplified version of Pavlova's "Dying Swan," and as soon as they get the snake arms right they should be able to dance the whole routine in toe shoes!

As yet another of my contributions to the honey industry, of which thine splendorous organization embodies the penultimate, I have written a training manual for all professionals who wish their apoidea to gain a faster and more orderly flight pattern when approaching and departing from their hives. This manual also explains how to install a banana peel landing platform, state-of-the-art skid preventer included, as well as instructions on how to introduce a mannerly system of waiting in line at entranceways, rather than the discourteous jockeying about that most workers seem to prefer but which wastes valuable time. This new system is sure to encourage less shilly-shallying and pay off handsomely with greater production, polite relationships, and improved morale.

There are other perceptive chapters on various ways to put drones to work, the transaction of painless sex changes, how to trick unproductive queens into being water boys, and an enlightening discourse on the unlikelihood of male bonding between females.

The last is a subject that somehow recalls the relationship between myself and thine errant Flatulence Second Class. Just yesterday evening, Sweets chugged over to my place in that rattletrap pickup of his and, after announcing his arrival with several of his smelly backfires, he swerved debonairly up my driveway, lost control, demolished my rhododendrons, and flattened a newly planted bed of marigolds. Blissfully unaware of the damage he had caused, he sat inside his pickup waiting for my apoidea (mispronounced by Sweets as "a poor idea") to go to sleep so that he could take a look at my new hives. In the meantime he inflicted me with one of his tiresome dissertations on the importance of protective garb and then went on and on about a painful experience of his when he was stung where his testicles would have been had they dropped.

By now the stars had come out. "Is it safe yet?" His Nibs asked.

After being assured that it was, he daintily stepped out

of his truck and cautiously peered around. Spotting a small moth in the distance, he hurriedly scrambled back in, uttering mouse-like squeaks while rolling up the windows. "Oh oh oh," he cried, "a bee!" "Never mind, Sweets honey," I said consolingly, "You can come out. I will protect you." "Well, maybe," he answered, adding primly, "but only if you open the door for me."

As usual, he was being my cross to bear. I contemplated giving the arrogant little twerp a good bop on the beezer, but then, for the sake of our male bonding, I managed to restrain myself. Opening the door, I complimented him on the three layers of netting he was sporting, and gently led him by the hand toward the hives. After several awkward stumbles he yanked back his hand and whined, "You forgot to smooth this path, didn't you!" "Well how would I have known you would be wearing your high heels'?" I inquired respectfully.

As we were inching nearer to the hives, he stopped short to check his veiling for holes and accused me of ignoring his previous command to clear away the brambles and cat briars. "We are not amused, not at all!" he squealed. His wrath was that of a pygmy rhinoceros and his flailing fingers resembled a spastic child's when playing an arpeggio on a toy harp. Stirred awake by his frantic motions, the sleeping hive became a black maelstrom of supersonic zooms and crisscrossings. "Help, help!" His Nibs screamed, veils flying as he hightailed it back to the safety of his truck.

O Honorable Royal Personages of OHEC, I only mention this incident as a single example of similar cross-bearing episodes. As valued a pal as your kinsman is, there are times when he forces me into positions that make me wonder if he is worth my affection. He sometimes makes me feel that I am responsible for some of the pea-brained things he does. I mean could I help it if he took my advice to convert that leaky old sailboat of his into a submarine? And when he did, how were we to know it would not come up'? And then when he comes over to visit it is like I am an unwanted guest in my own house. After sending me to the garage he plays marbles with my jelly beans and then eats up every one of them. I know he is just being childish whenever he cries over losing his security blanket, or that he is just being vengeful when he makes fun of my marvelous inventions and impressive awards. But maybe he will grow up. Perhaps thou can do something with him. I certainly hope so because, in spite of it all, I still value our bonding.

I do solemnly swear to the foregoing statements, so help me Allah, and do respectfully submit this reapplication for OHEC membership with salubrious salaams, prostrate genuflections, and continued wishes for thine Excellencies' good health. May thine camels never spit upon thou.

Thine most obedient servant,

former Grub,
Paul

HOW TO TELL BALLET
FROM MODERN

Unlike modern dance, ballet is the kind of thing you keep thinking will turn into something worth watching. In ballet everything is done with stiff necks, locked knees, and limp wrists, and it's all just one dainty position after another. And, as if that isn't bad enough, between poses there's a lot of tiptoeing, mostly with the dancers looking over their shoulder as if admiring themselves in a mirror, or maybe afraid the audience will go away. Personally, I wish they'd cut it out. It's the kind of stuff you want to keep your eyes off of. On the other hand, modern dancers move bigger and braver, have plenty of fluidity, in fact look like beautiful anacondas in heat. You know, lots of goo. And you don't have to worry about them breaking their necks either. But mostly they resemble human beings, whereas ballet dancers tend to be cute little windup toys with maddening birdlike squeaks, which are forgivable—not because of bird brains, but due to the rosin they have to keep rubbing on their toe shoes.

You can always tell ballet dancers by the length of their poses. The thoughtful type stay there long enough to give the critics time to trade opinions. This eats up a lot of time, but if you listen closely you can pick up some French while you wait, since all ballet steps are imported from Europe and referred to in French, unlike modern steps, which are homegrown American and have yet to be given any names at all. This is why most dance critics seem sunk in a swamp when it comes to describing modern dance. But nobody can blame them. You take their tags and labels away and what've they got? Not that modern is indescribable, it's just that maybe we should start looking to poets or even sportswriters to describe it.

Now, because they eat them, but mostly because of their steps, the French are called frogs or froggies, and ballet dancers are always doing those same old frog steps because if they didn't they wouldn't be doing ballet. It must be awful to get stuck in such a rut. The only times those poor souls get to do anything interesting is when their rosin doesn't work and they fall down. Otherwise, they tend to look like carbon copies of each other, not to mention their dances looking so repetitious and decorative. But it's easy to tell one modern dance from the other. As a rule, each grows organically out of itself in different ways, just as different types of fruit grow in nature, and each dancer looks like nobody else but himself (or herself). Individualism is encouraged, see.

It's perfectly okay not to be a clone. As for dainty dancing, the moderns would rather be caught dead. And you can always count on them heading in interesting new directions without falling down or getting stuck in one spot.

Nevertheless, we have to admit that ballet does have three things going for itself, namely:

It's harmless.
It's politically correct.
It's nothing to get upset over.

Anyone can appreciate ballet—politicians, the moral majority, redneck tree-top trimmers, drunks, women drivers, anybody. It's a regular idiot's delight.

Modern is more challenging, but highly rewarding to people who make the effort, plus the tickets are relatively inexpensive. It also presents a challenge to newspaper critics by causing them to think, which is good for them but usually results in missed deadlines.

And then there's this other thing that's catching on like wildfire abroad. It's called modern ballet, which is not only oxymoronic but plain moronic. Many dance nuts go for it, Croatians and Mongolians for instance, and especially the natives of Perth Amboy, who only heard about it last week over satellite communication. Well, what you look for in this mongrel species is cockamamie ballet steps done between total and unadulterated mess. Evidently, the modern ballet choreographer wishes to look like the last word in bees knees and is copying some up-to-date something he saw somewhere, only he doesn't quite remember what and has to fake it. Balanchine, a famous Russian, was one of these guys who made practically a whole career out of reinventing the flexed foot.

Now far be it from me to knock poor ignorant ballet people, or even critics—after all, fancy dancing is their bread and butter—but just to set everybody easy in their minds about telling ballet from modern, the main thing is to know that if there was just modern around we would never have another trouble in the world.

IN THE MARCEL PROUST SUITE
OF L'HOTEL CONTINENTAL

P ut the mirror down there. No, there, you dolt! Yes, there. Now put the other one there. Dear Lord, do I have to do everything myself? What's the matter with you, Spike? Hmm, I think I like my left profile best. Now tell me something. Which is best, my left or my right? Really, do you think so? I'm not so sure. Maybe the left is better. Oh, why can't you agree with everything I say?

What do you think you're getting paid for anyway? And another thing I've been meaning to mention. Equerries are supposed to bow respectfully with the tops of their heads presented, not their rear ends. Got that? Jeeze!

Now look, we've got to get this seating plan for the gala celebration following my induction into the Legion straightened out once and for all. I told you I do NOT wish to sit next to that fruity Pierre Cardin. I want our American ambassador's wife. Either her or their Airedale. Oh, all right, have it your own way. But no cats.

Yes, I hear you. It is very important, also very natural, that the French perceive me as being wholesomely American. Don't worry, you won't catch me being photographed in my French-cut underwear. Once this thing is over you won't catch me in Paris anymore either, for that matter. In any case this uniform with the tingly gold epaulets becomes me. I don't wish to be thought of as a mere millionaire or career diplomat. It is true that I am the embodiment of the American ideal, possibly even more so than Clinton himself. Only without Monica. By the way, we must arrange it so that the French president always sees me from a lower position. I must always be higher than he and his subjects. Make a note to send someone round the city to find the best balconies. What? I shouldn't use balconies anymore? Well, how could I help falling? That stupid railing was weak, that's all.

Now write this down: no cats at my induction ceremony. No *CATS*, got it? I can't stand the way they stare at me. And during the ceremony I want all our dancers to be standing at attention in a truly straight line for a change. Tell them no yawning or sloppy slouching. What's more, they are to be holding books in their hands. *Tarzan and the Jewels of Opar* will do. We are not going to be illiterate philistines. Is that clear?

And what is this I hear about our boys getting into fist fights with the Air France stewards on the way over? I simply won't have them fraternizing with Frogs. Who came out on top? I want it investigated. And another thing, how's about this for our new Company slogan: To Dance Is to Hit Hard. Very good, I'm sure you'll agree. And here's an even better one: We Dance Softly and Carry a Big Stick. What, it's already been used? Perhaps it's not so good.

Now make another note while I can still remember it. I want a company salary freeze to keep inflation under control, but we are to increase Halloween bonuses by one hundred percent. No, I don't think the latter will cancel out the effects of the former. How dare you doubt it! How many times do I have to prove to you my masterful grip on economics? And something else: We are not to tip any more bellhops here. They've flatly refused to walk Rover, said he tended to crap on their feet. A likely story. Rover would never do any such ungentlemanly thing.

Is my Foreign Legion medal going to be pretty? It's not the Foreign Legion, only Legion of Honor? Rats, and here I thought they'd be letting me ride a camel and lead ground forces into North Africa. I may give the medal to Rover. Perhaps he would like to wear it on his collar.

What, they are here for the ceremony already? Hurry, help me with this plumed helmet. That's right, now go send them straight in. You may wait in the hall. I don't want you contradicting me during my acceptance speech like last time.

Good evening, madams and masseurs. Do come in. I must say that it is a great pleasure to accept this honor from . . . uh, what did you say your name was? Oh, President Milreaux. Of course you are. How are all your troubles with the Brits going? And how is your Minister of Finance son-in-law? It is always good to keep government in the family, so to speak.

Hey, watch it! Oh, now I see. The kisses were just a formality. Mr. President, sir, I shall wear this well-deserved medallion with pride. Please thank all the wise and tasteful officials who decided to give it to me, won't you? OK, everybody, that's it. Don't forget to take your umbrellas on the way out.

Spike, you may come back in now. Thank God that's over. Fetch me a Kleenex to wipe with, will you? That president drools, and I couldn't understand one word he was saying. You'd think these people could learn some English.

Now where were we? Oh yes, the reservation for my flight home. I don't care where I sit, just so it's first class and right behind the pilots' compartment with the door open. I just love all those little dashboard doodads and blinky lights and stuff. If I show them my medal do you think they might let me drive? Remember how I drove the helicopter over the Berlin Wall and accidentally pulled on the wrong lever that made us end up in Albania with no wheels? That was planchettian fun, was it not? Remind me to include it in my next autobiography. I said planchettian. Oh never mind.

What is that thing staring at me? Who let that cat in here? Since when have we had a company cat? Spike, you idiot, you know I can't stand cats! What do you mean it saves on mousetraps? Don't tell me when I can or cannot use my Saturday night special indoors. Put your hands over your ears and stand back or you'll get shot too!

Oh dear, I don't feel well. I'm a sensitive person, Spike honey. This is not good for my artistic temperament; I shouldn't have to look at all this blood and mess. Get the maids to clean it up.

What do you mean it's not dead yet? Take it out and wring its neck. No, I don't want to do it myself. Uh oh, I'm going to be sick. Hand me that vase quick. No, not that tacky thing, the Ming one.

Now write this down and keep on reminding me: This is absolutely the last time we are ever staying at any hotels anywhere with cats running around in them and that's that.

FANTASY ABOUT
JOINING THE CIA

In Porto Alegre, after many lecture-demonstrations, parties, and other nuisances, something happens that at first seems to provide a reason for my mixing-up of people; but later, when examining the problem further, reviewing what happened—in fact, when being confronted with the whole of my past—I grow more duplicitous than ever. By revealing this curious occurrence I may be called a liar, or perhaps only an inventor of riddles; yet, after all, an artist is supposed to make riddles out of answers.

Among interesting people met at State Department functions have been U.S. Secret Service personnel. One of them has told me that Nazis are still nesting there in Argentina, and this leads me to dream of serving my country in another, less public and more adventurous way. So I cable the CIA in Washington, pointing out the ideal cover that my position as cultural ambassador could provide, but, though I fill out the formal application that they send and mail it back in an improvised diplomatic pouch marked Do Not Bend, they reject me due to, of all things, a past history of traffic violations. This is hard to accept. Greenwich Village has been rigidly enforcing a code against jaywalking, but I've hardly ever been caught. It seems more likely that the rejection is due to some psychiatric disorder that mistakenly got into my dossier. Subsequently, after obtaining a clean bill of health from a gentleman I mistake for a Peruvian Zen master (he turned out to be a teacher of the tea ceremony) and digesting several books on weaponry, since my knowledge of missiles has been limited to the pea shooters and spitballs of boyhood, I reapply. Nevertheless, I am again rejected.

My interest in spying, incidentally, has led to a passion for mechanical things—handheld heaters in particular. By '66 I amassed a collection of pistols that included two loud Colts with doodads that spun. I called these Lovey and Dovey, my twin birds of doom. They were excellent for scaring off studio intruders, and once I shot up a nest of roaches that had settled behind the studio's toilet tank, nearly drowning myself.

Well, you can imagine my excitement when, in an answer to a third application, my diplomatic pouch is returned all starched and ironed. Although there is no communication inside, this is obviously Washington's way of telling me they accept me as being straight and that I shall soon be given an assignment. At last I am to start a new double life which will change me into a secret agent!

My first brush with Intelligence occurs on the evening of June 10, 1965, at approximately twenty-two hours, and coincides with a devastating hurricane, which whips all the way up from Cape Horn to semitropical Porto Alegre, bringing monstrous icebergs that squeeze the bejesus out of that port's tankers, sloops, and children's inflatable rafts. The company and I have just finished our first and only performance at the Teatro Salao de Atos de Urgs (pronounce "Urghzz," with a soft lisp of the Portuguese rolled *r*), and rain, ruin, and loud pops are reigning outside.

While I am greeting a shivering throng of after-performance admirers, warming them with my smile, our ambassador arrives. As usual, he is tall and wholesome looking. I crouch in politeness to allow his head to be at the preferred level and present my palm after demoisturizing it on the back of my tights. But just as we are sharing the familiar knuckle-shattering scrunch, he is hustled away by several armed backstage guards.

Evidently, he was not who he seemed.

Persevering, I start over with the true ambassador, who has been waiting directly behind the other. This man is unusually short for an ambassador and is displaying a tight, many-buttoned puce uniform which he certainly never could have put on by himself. He arches back and glides forward, hugs affectionately at my waist, and then, with an air of secrecy, slips me an envelope sealed with a waxen crest.

The angels have chosen to net for me my rapturous dreams of Central Intelligence!

I can barely wait to run to the men's room, memorize my instructions, then destroy them—can already hear the merry sound of flushing. But the hairnet he is wearing WOULD get caught in the front zipper of my costume, and until some guards can unmesh us, I while away a considerable amount of time by dreaming of Col. Adjutant Pawl Tälürr, aerial double agent to outer space, who at ninety-three is to be one of the solar system's greatest narcs ever. Photographers flash away, their used bulbs bouncing onto the stage and mingling there with other discards—the broken bouquets, crinkled tubes of liniment, and what may have been the prone body of an exhausted curtain puller with the cord of one of Bet's dehumidifiers snaking out from beneath.

Suddenly the tall, wholesome man strides back, leading a battalion of plainclothesmen who carelessly yank the little ambassador from my zipper, doing in the hairnet forever. What seems a heartless act then turns into something else. A chloroformed cloth is produced and clamped over the little man's unprotesting mouth, and as he is being bound and borne away to a torture cell, a moonlit wall, who knew where—I am able to assure him with a wink that his directives will be obeyed.

When I sneak a look inside the envelope, however, it

contains only a disappointing invitation to another reception. The tall man then whacks at my back, introduces himself with a foreign-sounding name that I am unable to catch, and congratulates me for the entrapment tactics that he thinks I have used. He says that he is the CIA's slipperiest customer, the last living descendant of Brazil's second-oldest family, a Soviet multiple agent, and none other than the very rich as well as childless and totally insane Senhor Saläo de Atos da Urgs himself. Does he mean the other man or himself, or whom?

Although the real ambassador has never come backstage at all, having been screened as a common autograph hound, and although I ponder the matter of identities for years, it is still unclear as to which man, the tall or the short, was Senhor Urgs. It is depressing. Was I responsible for the incarceration of one of my own government's agents?

The glossy prints of the enlarged photos depicting the entire entrapment are discovered by my company archivist in a trunk where they have been lying among the tatters of a faded red-and-blue costume. Eventually I find the pictures so unsettling that I destroy them. In some I was able to make out the shoulders of the three of us, but our faces were a white blur. The reflection of my smile had overexposed things. But in the penultimate one of the series, taken just as the short man was being bound and borne away, I could distinctly see his arm being raised toward me in triumph and reassurance.

DEATH WISH

Folks, at times such as when thoughts of lust and disorder upset me and keep me awake, I play this game—just a game.

You're airborne, sailing effortlessly, gliding in an upward arc, then riding the crest of the world's greatest leap. There are trees below, Norway spruce at first, then honey locusts blending into mimosas, eucalyptus, and then royal palms; and way down there, gathered in glades, too far away to hear but near enough to see, are clusters of people waving welcome banners, and their upturned lips shape into pretty little smiles; and in the long length of that leap you pass over more such clusters, sometimes rosy people, sometimes shining black, and farther on, people of varied pigmentations, all with smiles of welcome; and you wonder how many more miles, and the soft air presses on your face. And you think—lucky, lucky to be welcome, and that it would be nice to rest your head on someone's shoulder or sleep with an arm around you. Yet there's no pause to that arc, no break at the crest of that neurol glide which is taking you to some unnamed place.

Maybe there have been no trees, no people—never mind, it doesn't matter much. Maybe an unpopulated countryside is stretching out below, a peaceful, starlit plain, and you're the one to see it first.

And so you sail and glide on and on.

And the plain slopes gradually up to a mountain chain, and the mountains slope gradually down to a sandy stretch, and the stretch slopes up, and you think you're getting the idea as to where you're headed. And then, sure enough, beyond some dunes is the turquoise sea, and you know that at last you're coming home, floating gently downward, breathing sighs at the beauty of the place. Starlit wavelets lap a gleaming shore. It's midsummer. It's dawn, the beginnings of a sunset in reverse. The night sky lightens, the sun peeps up. Suddenly, everything's all-over pink.

Leaving their nestless eggs lying unprotected on the sand, snowy terns run their beaks along the surface of the sea. Below, waving blades of eel grass shelter multicolored minnows and—oh, why not?—an admirable, large blue shark.

And now it's exactly noon. The moment has come to unwind your Ace bandage or throw off your clothes or donate your old truss to a museum, and the salty sea is just great for whatever ails you and you're about to have your lovely noontime dip.

You drop right in. A light caress. The water's deep, but not so deep that you can't see the bands of sandy furrows far below, dappled by dancing lights, and you let yourself sink down and down, and there you are on the bottom, stretched out comfortably, arms crossed at your chest.

Ah, that's better. The day was getting glary. From far above, the sun's now cooler light shines in long shafts through the sea.

No, this mustn't be. No, it's not time yet. Dear God of All Order, please delay this leap.

TRICKS OF THE TRADE

Making up a dance is like writing a poem,
Only words have little to do with it.
The only words you may need are ones to shout
At your dancers if they don't cooperate.

And, like all poets do, you start by buying
Several bottles of booze and cartons of cigs.
These will make your job seem like fun, easy as pie,
Even give the illusion of knowing what you are doing.

So then you round up some gullible dancers
And urge them into a rehearsal studio.
They will be eager for you to show them some steps,
But you won't need to think up any yet.

What you do is sit in a comfortable chair, have a drink
And smoke until a thick cloud fills the studio.
Someone will ask you to open the windows, which you do,
Because the profession requires you to make minor sacrifices.

Pretty soon you find that somebody has hidden your ashtray.
You excuse yourself and go out to buy another,
Telling everyone to invent some steps while you are away.
But you don't go shopping. That was just a trick.

You go to the studio of an ex-dancer of yours
Who has been making dances of his own,
And you find, just as you knew you would,
That he has filched some of your steps.

Since you never remember any of your steps,
You select the best ones and video them.
Be sure to thank your ex-dancer for stealing your stuff,
Seeing as imitation is the highest form of flattery.

Back at your studio you show the video to your dancers.
Only they prefer to do their own steps, which can be
Somewhat discouraging. This is when having another drink
Will make it possible to go on having lots of fun.

By the way, be sure not to let all this enjoyment
Go beyond reason. Injuries may occur when you demonstrate steps
Or when using the palm of your hand for an ashtray.
Always keep a first aid kit, ice pack, and crutches handy.

Then there's the matter of what you should wear.
It's a well-known fact that anyone in charge
Should dress differently than his underlings, such as a
High-class getup with large medallions and plumed helmet.

I learned this from the Queen of England
When attending a dance concert with her.
She wore a vintage dress of an unforgettable type
That went out of fashion about fifty years ago.

The next step in the Creative Process
Is to retreat to some less distracting place.
You need a little time by yourself.
It is not too late to form a workable plan.

The bathroom, roof, or squeezing inside
The broom closet should do it.
Undisturbed, you will come up with the
Architectural shape of your wonderful new dance.

If the music has already been chosen,
You can follow its structure. If not,
The shape of a cantaloupe, cucumber,
Or even a gunny sack will do nicely.

Should none of these shapes appeal to you
Or if your imagination is limited,
Do not worry, something will come to you.
What you can't visualize is what you'll get.

If you allow your mind to dwell on structure,
You may want the form to follow the function,
But everyone knows that a dance has no use,
So why worry about it?

Now you may be asking the chicken-or-egg question,
Which comes first, the steps or the music?
It's simple. First comes the money.
Studio rentals are not cheap.

Anything you wish to communicate is quite acceptable.
Take your ideas in stride, don't let them disturb you.
Trust in the perceptiveness of those who watch,
Let them figure out your dance for themselves.

Lastly, about a certain technicality—the recurring confusion
Over left and right. You must trust the dancers to
Know which foot is which, and even if they don't,
There's no need to get involved with such fine points.

Stay loose, think pink, have another drink.
Count the minutes until your dancers
Will be off on tour and out of your hair.
Maybe they will send you pretty postcards.

THERE IS A TIME
A lyric for Don York

There is a time for everything,
A time for everything under the sun.
Take dogs, for instance.
Every dog has its day, they say.
Or take dance, for instance.
Some dance looked better yesterday.

happy woo woos,
doo doos, las, etc.
may be inserted
anywhere

There is a time for everything,
Time for everything under the sun.
Yesterday I was nuts about dance.
Yesterday, last week, and then some.

You know how it is when you love somebody a lot
For a long long time
And then they get old and lose their looks
But you love them even more
Because now you know
It wasn't just their looks you were after.
Well, that is not the way I feel about dance
At the present moment.

a la recitativ

There is a time for everything,
Time for everything under the sun.
The wintertime sun is telling me come,
Come and love dance once more.
Each morning I get up and say
I'll go crazy for dance today.
Today I'll go nuts for sure.

Then back in my bed I say, oh, well,
Tomorrow I'll have to try harder. Hell,
Tomorrow I'm sure to love dance real quick.
Tomorrow I'll even love music.

There is a time for everything,
Time for everything under the sun.
And dance will again be like life. It will.
And dogs will again have their day.
It's a far better thing to rise hopeful
Than to stay in bed all day, they say, or bay
through the long winter nights. That's right.
It's a far better thing to like life
Than to lump it, they say
they say, some say,
no lumping they say,
they say, some say
no lumping they say
say they, some so say, so they ... aw nuts

spooky
echo effect
here

LIMERICK FOR
JENNIFER TIPTON*

For beautiful Jennifer Tip
To pack in her dainty tool kit.
All know beyond doubt
That when touring about
She loves to both light and get lit.

*Ever since 1966 the highly acclaimed Jennifer Tipton has designed the lighting for the majority of my dances. This limerick went with a bottle of vodka that I gave her on the premiere of my dance *Orbs*.

THE LAST THUMP

O Great Puppeteer, untangler of strings.
Old sleight-of-hand prankster upstairs,
Thanks for sheltering wings
And other good things
Such as soft boards and hard derrieres.

And thanks for our yogurts, the vitamin Cs,
The gray tablets of powdered beef liver,
For ice packs that freeze,
Hot hydrotherapies,
And for paddings on knees all aquiver.

But very few thanks for the light board gone wrong
When the pit becomes perilously murky.
Our flaccid swan song
Doesn't take all that long.
Why this short-running flop, this quick turkey?

Yet Your satisfied sighs when Your plans finalize
At the sound of our ponderous kerplops
Reveal a rule awfully wise,
Though a shocking surprise
To us chumps who get dumped on our rumps.

Dust-dimmed our doomed eyes then lift up to the flies,
Far beyond the bright stage that we quit.
But our unending cries
In such gladness arise
As we sit in the pit where we hit,

For our followers know that we're ever to be
Unperturbed by the curtain's last thump.
Though board-bound, we're string-free,
Unimpounded, You see,
Even things in the night that go bump.

LOVE IS A DOG FROM HELL

Feet of fluff
Killer teeth
Nose that hates menthol cigs
Eyes like a Tasmanian devil

He prefers his own puke
Is bored with mice
Is docile when drunk
Pisses at everything

Is superficial at Sit!
And Stay! and Roll over!
And totally ignores Stop that!
And smells bad

His ears have become stale
They require fumigating
With his very own can of air freshener
(Potpourri Country Fields, 99 cents)
He disdains it
Hides his muzzle
You have to rope
His mouth shut

I can no longer sleep
He claws the bedclothes
Takes up all the room
And jerks in his dreams

There is grumbling under the comforter
But as yet no biting
Something is hopping across my face
His fleas are relocating

Dear old Dee Dee dog
Where did you go?
And Jake and Blackie and Emma?
Them was good doggies

Devil eyes
Shredded sheets
Machine gun claws
This whole marriage is ridiculous

POGGIE IN THE QUIET,
BY CLEAVE YARNS

Already, even before the City Center curtain rose, the nerves in our toes began to tingle and the muscles in our abdomen started to knot. The Playbill informed us that Peter Poggie was to be performing the world premiere of a solo to Debussy's "La Mer" adapted for bo's'ns' whistle but, due to difficulties with the bo's'ns' union, would be rendered on a harpsichord by George H. Tacet, Ph.D., who was also credited with the choreography, costume, lighting, makeup, and hairstyling. Dr. Tacet's name was prominently displayed in gigantic lettering, he being someone who not only is multi-talented but, presumably, has pull with the printer. The costume turned out to be the bottom half of thrift-shop pajamas sewn with a staggering number of sea green sequins which made Mr. Poggie resemble an overly scaled mermaid or glittery porpoise.

To be perfectly aboveboard, we must admit that Mr. Poggie, in spite of his fishy-looking getup, is the essence of a man—not too dominating, mind you, but with an admirably constructed escarpamezzo,* which, by the way, he does not allow to be photographed. He is also blessed with an abundance of self-assurance, which is a prerequisite of any artist, second only to an omniscience that tells him to set aside a day, an hour, or even less time to get in shape, practice stressful new steps, and solve the riddle of wrapping his ailing left ankle with an Ace bandage; the type of wisdom, in short, that owes much to past experience, the heartbreaks of torn tendons, and such. However, Mr. Poggie's ability to perform in spite of injury probably owes more to his psychiatrist than to the aforesaid omniscience. Be that as it may, the most important prerequisite for any artist is that his performances be explained to a mystified public by highly discerning reviewers such as myself.

After the house lights dimmed, causing several late-comers to briefly lower themselves into my lap, the grand

---

*The *New International Dictionary* seems to be somewhat confused over this word, saying that it has been derived from the Old Scandinavian root or perhaps the Middle Indonesian, one of which may refer to the lower digestive system. This is as close as it comes to what we have in mind here. However, it then goes on to say that an escarpamezzo could be related to the small bumps on a cucumber. This is close, yet still not right. But then, if you let your eyes drift downward only an inch or so on the page, you will be somewhat enlightened by finding the word eschatology, a branch of archaeology known for the study of large Egyptian stelae.

drape rose to reveal the shadowy presence of Mr. Poggie, who happened to be standing just beyond the outside rim of a bright circular pool of light. But then, having quickly corrected his spacing, he became quite visible. There he was: essence, omniscience, bare feet and all. Alas, the harpsichord had not been delivered on time and he was just standing there in the quiet. Time was also standing still, as rigid as a popsicle, as inactive as a stuffed mongoose. We consulted our watch. Would he never move or was he counting the house? Whatever, he was certainly building our expectations.

At long last he moved. After turning around to face up-stage, Mr. Poggie introduced the dance's subject matter with a naturalistic gesture. That is, when we saw him tug down the seat of his costume we gathered that the dance was to be a universal ode to fundamentals, or to the world prior to cultural refinement, or to life in general, or something along those lines. As perplexing as metaphors can be, Mr. Poggie is often open-ended. We, for one, wished that he would face front again and let us have another view of his interestingly shaped escarpamezzo. We, for another, disagree with those who say it is too small.

Having stated his theme, he then executed several of the best serpentos d'Egyptae that this writer has ever seen anywhere, ones transpiring so rapidly that one could not be sure of the exact number. The effect was that of spaghetti gone haywire. As a relief, he then launched into a single boca l'silencio, which, roughly translated from the Spanish, means cow in the quiet. We regret to say that it was some-what less than grade A. Our readers who are familiar with the step can appreciate the technical virtuosity required for this highly stylized form of tiptoeing.

It was not that Mr. Poggie's execution lacked definition, or that the choice of animal imagery was out of context; it was only that he did not lift his knees cautiously or high enough between shifts of weight, and his feet came down much too forcefully. In fact the execution of the stepping, from the constricted beginnings to the slapdash conclusions, was rather disappointing. As anyone who has ever attended to cattle can attest, this is not how cows tiptoe. It was just wrong. But try to tell him that.

As all we dance lovers know, and eventually learn to live with, Mr. Poggie when airborne has a curious tendency to whistle midair. This time his shrill piping sounded like a tone-deaf Baptist's rendition of "Jesus Loves Me," which in-dicated a certain talent for rhythmic accuracy, yet that abil-ity was neglected when indulging in essentially arid surges of a declamatory nature, ones best typified by the recurrent, "Oh, I'm full of it tonight!" But, to be fair, there was an im-mediacy here that, if inelegant, was pleasantly informal, as were several other impromptu utterances. Most leaps were preceded by, "Here goes again, folks!" and all landings ac-companied by a small but audible grunt. One could wish the soaring heights of his elevations were achieved at less expense in the way of a more graceful flow of vocalization.

Not to digress, but this seems as good a place as any to

notify our many faithful readers that they may henceforth find our reviews located elsewhere, in as the publisher of this periodical, faced with declining sales and determined to increase advertisement space, has banned all run-on sentences with subordinate clauses inserted, which is a heartless restriction that we are unable to approve.

To continue with this, my final effort to contribute cultural enlightenments to these pages: unlike Mr. Poggie's boca l'silencio, his pas l'piscados were particularly fish-like, and his flambo d'bombas nothing short of incendiary. Pausing between each of these thrilling marvels, graciously allowing connoisseurs enough time to trade opinions, he then treated us to the spectacular mort du canard, towards which all of us had been yearning. The takeoff and height were scrupulously correct, the descent somewhat less so. Indeed, it somehow reminded us of the skid landing of a jetliner whose pilot had neglected to lower the wheels. Yet Mr. Poggie was up in a flash, pausing only long enough to assure himself that he had completely recovered the use of his limbs.

Having startled us with these and other forms of levitation, he then became less airy and more grounded or, as nature lovers would endorse, ecology-oriented. It was as if dark forces of gravity were driving him into the bowels of the earth. He seemed exceedingly enamored of dirt, plowed his chest through it, intently traveling around and around by means of a rippling use of his stomach muscles, perhaps inspired by the looping movements of an inchworm or some other natural wonder, rather than the sterile stasis of corrugated cardboard. This was a newly invented step (the pas d'écologie, if I may be so bold as to christen it). Indeed, it may be Dr. Tacet's most lasting gift to present and future generations of balletomanes. Seeing Mr. Poggie ripple along like that, his jaw distended with frightful significance, his beetled brow inclined ominously, gave one the distinct impression of the gluttonous larvae of moths that dine on our woolens. Speaking of insects, it has been reported that the many pet tarantulas Mr. Poggie keeps have intercepted his footsteps for so long that his gait can be compared to that of a man wading through low surf. This particular characteristic, however, need not be a restriction to the full enjoyment of his dancing, as it was barely noticeable throughout this performance.

The solo was rounded off with a cunningly enlarged permutation of the opening move—i.e., the seat-revealing exposition, or might this be termed a reposition? When dazzled by the shifting sun rays of multi-layered art we humbly admit to uncertainty. Architecturally speaking, one might compare the solo's overall shape to that of an eggplant. At any rate, whatever the structure was, one was left with the doubled satisfaction of completeness combined with relief.

The heavy grand drape descended, slowly at first, then in fits and starts as if reluctant to close the gap between us and Mr. Poggie. Gaining speed, it smacked the boards and was eclipsed by an apotheosis of dust followed by politely muffled coughs and sneezes, a silent span of discomfort, and then the theatre was rent with tumult—thunderbolt sounds of rushing feet that were headed towards the exits. We of the fourth estate lingered briefly while shouting, "Bellas Tardes!" We had been astounded, stunned, overwhelmed. United by analogous reactions to the dust, handkerchiefs pressed to our noses, we suppressed our conflicting opinions of the concert, interlocked arms, and quietly escorted one another out. Bound together by mutual discomfort, it was almost as if we had been the victims of a shared disaster.

Mr. Poggie, known for maintaining his omniscient self-assurance at all odds, is likely to have taken many a noble bow in the empty silence.

THE SHIRLEY TEMPLE MURDERS

Chapter One

Call me Ishmael, for that is the name I use here in Purcyville at this time. Some years ago, having made a quick retreat from the monotony of my hometown to start a new chapter of my life in the resort area of Death Valley, I went by the name of Lazarus. Subsequently, when signing the register at a decrepit Nantucket inn with walls about to tumble down, it seemed appropriate to use the name Joshua. In Perth Amboy, having grown tired of being so biblical, I changed my surname to Rose, although "Mr. Stinky" was what a certain inhospitable landlady called me behind my back. But what did that matter? As everyone knows, a rose by any other name would smell as sweet. I have gone by these and other aliases in many towns and villages where my lust for travel requires me to be. But why, you may well ask, must I keep traveling from one locality to another, and to each under a different name? What do I have against settling down within a single environment where people would be aware of my true identity? Simply put, I find that presenting a new face to each new place is satisfying, perhaps as fulfilling as when a professional actor feels he has triumphed over a variety of demanding roles. Yet I am no actor, and my masquerades are only entertaining little games played in order to avoid the repetitiousness of a sedentary life.

Now, when I say that I am in the habit of traveling from one place to another, I do not mean that I ever go as a mere tourist. No, I take up a residency at each community in order to survey mankind, to see how it ticks, to plumb its depths and, more tellingly, to wade its shallows. Sometimes when I relate to the attractive people I meet it seems as if I am a bedazzled Narcissus reaching down for his own reflection. The risk of drowning is the main attraction, since one needs to recognize that mirrored image, the ungraspable phantom of life, as well as its shimmering shadow of death, to both of which all adventurers are drawn. This is the duple magnet that can be the key to my story.

But it is unusual for me to play any sort of active role in the neighborhoods where my investigations take me, and I rarely involve myself in any way with community events. In most ways my entire life has been that of a background person, an observer rather than a participant. I am in the habit of exploring issues from multiple sides, weighing all facets of the human animal one against another, then drawing my own conclusions. Admittedly, my judgment is fallible and I am apt to change my mind several times in the process; in fact I may never reach any solutions at all, but the puzzling is what keeps my solitary life from being dull.

I could not believe it at the time but have since come to realize that what Purcyville's most untrustworthy gossips were saying was entirely true. Yet how could anything so unusual occur in such a safe and uneventful village? How could it have happened, and why in the world would anyone want to do such a thing? Never before had I heard of such sad deaths, not even that of the local party caterer who, on a windy day, climbed to the top of a tall tree to remove a balloon caught in its branches, reached too far, and fell, the wayward balloon still bobbing gaily; or the elderly Washington Beltway driver with a weak bladder who unintentionally caused a whole chain of fatal accidents during rush hour by suddenly stopping his car in the fast lane in order to use his sorely needed urine container, one kept handy for such emergencies, but which was already full—not that it mattered afterwards.

Over the years, *Redneck Life*, Loudoun County's most popular weekly, has covered other deaths: the child who died of hypothermia from being force-fed ice cream nonstop in order keep her quiet; the curious little boy who, intending to drink from the bottle that his alcoholic mother kept hidden among her cleaning materials, swallowed muriatic acid instead; the final aria of Alfonso Magdelenus, an elephantine operatic tenor with a defective larynx who, when attacked by loud boos from the audience, strode toward the wings with dignity, tripped on an uneven board, crashed into the pin rail, and bounced back onto the stage, where he screeched in a register that only dogs could have heard, while being fatally crushed by a quickly dropped front curtain; the baby twins whose simultaneous deaths by suffocation occurred due to their loving mother's prolonged hugging of them, her breasts as effective as a pair of down pillows; the ignoble passing of an unidentified derelict whose body was discovered inside the locked stall of a toilet for the handicapped, the cardboard tube from a roll of used-up toilet paper still clutched in his hand.

There are certain residents of Purcyville, of course, who insist on making jokes about such pitiful deaths, always very corny jokes, yet, to my knowledge, no one has had cheek enough to speak lightly about what has lately happened to poor little Shirley.

She had been given her supper, coaxed into her Doctor Dentons (much whining over the troublesome feet), and put to bed early. Her parents, other members of the family, and a guest who happens to be a confidant of mine were sitting around the dinner table when they heard a shot that came from upstairs. The father did not get up at once, but sat paralyzed for four or five heartbeats, his mouth stuffed with pig-in-a-blanket, not daring to chew or swallow, much less spit it into his napkin, and when he did get up, having realized that he had left his hunting gun out in plain view where his beloved four-year-old daughter might have discovered it, he dashed up the stairs. Those who followed him into the nursery noticed that when he spotted a small, bloody hole in Shirley's left temple both of his hands flew up to press against his own temples, and he kept switching the mouthful of pig-in-a-blanket from one cheek to the other, still unable to decide what to do with it.

Purcyville, a small community in Virginia, had been an excellent choice for my present investigations. Having motored south from Boston, the first indication of what my new environment would be like was at a grassy area dotted with Dixie cups and other trash beside Route No. 7, a minor highway that connects Winchester, Virginia, to Washington, D.C. It was there that I noticed that a sign indicating the turnoff to Purcyville had been defaced. Someone, a local no doubt, had crossed out the village's name and scrawled the words KEEP GOING with angry red paint. Although Mrs. Robey, who I later learned was Purcyville's unpopular bastion of cultural uplift, highly disapproved of the sign's disfigurement, the rest of the residents applauded it. They valued their isolation from "furren" day trippers, Richmond swells included, and took excessive pride in it. Highfalutin city slickers should stay where they belonged, for Purcyville was to remain a tight little territory that neither wanted nor needed anything from strangers.

The townsfolk also disagreed with Mrs. Robey over the matter of the off-color bumper stickers, particularly the ones that said, "It's not how you pick your nose, it's where you put the boogers," and when she tried to have them removed from Dobson's Drugstore, Mr. Dobson simply relocated them to a more frequented place by the condoms. What Mrs. Robey had not realized was that those particular stickers could encourage a certain type of social refinement among Purcyville's numerous nose pickers, at least the ones who could read.

And then there was Mrs. Robey's mania for banning books, even though residents rarely used the library of which she was the sole owner and entire Board of Trustees. First she had withdrawn all the volumes with the word brassiere in them, then all medical textbooks with anatomical illustrations were replaced with an "educational" series about the Bobbsey Twins. Inspired by the stirring fundamentalist outpourings of Reverend Hooker, she had begun door-to-door collections to raise funds for the addition of a new wing to her library that would hold nothing but expurgated Bibles written in words easily grasped by the most backward of local inhabitants. There seemed to be no end to Mrs. Robey's betterment efforts, but little did anyone know of the coming homicide or of the evil heart that hid behind her holier-than-thou exterior.

* * *

It was a peculiarly spring-like day during the Christmas holidays when I first strolled the short block of Purcyville's main street, a narrow one-way affair that is cloyingly entitled Love Lane. The sky was clear, the air wonderfully mild with merely a slight edge of frost to it. The earsplitting whistle of a passing train was tapering to a whisper—a welcome relief lent by the enchantment of distance. As was usual, there had been no reason to stop for any alien passengers to get off. Dressed lightly, gossiping townsfolk were gathered in tight clusters, most of the men wearing Rotary T-shirts, penny loafers, and beaked Budweiser caps. Bordering the street were establishments likely to furnish nearly everything that anyone would ever need: grocery, dry goods, drug and hardware stores, bank, barber shop, sidewalk café (a single sip of its curious version of coffee was all I could manage), police station, and a firehouse that partly blocked the view of a seedy house of ill-fame with a flashing neon sign that wrongly identified it as being a tavern. Both sides of the street were lined with fresh Christmas trees decorated with slapdash chains of paper rings, ones evidently made by butterfingered grade schoolers. On closer inspection I discovered that most of these chains were supplied with a tag bearing their maker's first name, and it both surprised and delighted me to know that there were so many, at least three, Shirleys involved. Which I assumed was due to their being namesakes of the currently popular movie tot known coast to coast as Shirley Temple. Oh, joy! Shirley was the very name that always brings back a rush of memories. Shirley, sweet Shirley, short little Shirley. One of these could be my very own, the long-lost child that continually inspires and directs me to the uppermost mission of my life.

*

When Sheriff O'Hoolihan and I first met—a chance encounter at Dobson's Drugstore—what I most noticed about him were his eyes. Depending on the light, they were pale or dark blue. Laugh lines fanned out from the corners, and I could not help but notice that the left eye was somewhat larger than the right. The eyelashes were long enough to be the envy of any woman but would probably be highly suspicious to any man, and what I took to be a flirtatious series of winks in fact turned out to be merely a tic. At times there was a mocking or ironic quality to the eyes, even if not intended; at other moments they sparkled with mischievousness or, when faced with an insolvable mystery (I had asked where the hemorrhoid suppositories were), they went blank and seemed to bask in a childlike blue lunacy. His eyes, therefore, were expressive, even though no expression was intended. They were also rather warm, or I should say anything but icy, and not once were they indifferent, which made me feel that I was worth their curiosity—lively eyes giving the immediate, if false, impression of being sympathetic to whatever person or object or scene they fixed upon. Yet, besides the animation, there was a paradoxical hint of bleak defense, a gloomy carapace, a protective cover. Perhaps the sheriff, out of necessity, was wearing invisible dark glasses to lessen the glare of unwelcome memories of past indiscretions, or even a sin or two. But only of the ordinary kind—sins of which we can all be guilty.

The second time Sheriff O'Hoolihan and I met it was not by chance. I had heard that little Shirley's death was far from being accidental, or so the grapevine had it, and I wanted to ask him if the rumor was true.

Looking distraught, he was pacing around in his small, well-kept office at the police station. The room was impressively neat, nothing out of place—writing paper, pencils, fountain pen, ink bottle—each object on his desk arranged precisely, or one might even say nitpickingly. The pristine white walls were a vision of purity, with the exception of a rude reddish stain that could have been caused by leakage of some sort. A framed travel poster had been hung as if with the aid of a carpenter's level. I had expected a wanted flyer or two but there were none. A water dish on the floor hinted of a fondness for dogs, and a flea-bitten mutt soon appeared from under the desk, sniffed my shoe, momentarily studied my proffered hand, then occupied itself with the more pressing matter of chewing at its rear end.

O'Hoolihan greeted me as if we were old friends, offered

me a chair, and plopped his heavyset body into the rickety seat behind his desk, causing it to squeak in loud protest. "Hey there, pal," he trumpeted, "what's cookin'?" "I know it is none of my business," I replied, "but I heard that little Shirley was not shot by her father's gun. Can it be that she was murdered?" Quickly shifting his eyes to the side and sounding annoyed, he said, "Yeah, her father's gun is a shotgun and the hole in his girl's head was from a single bullet. I'm all at sixes and sevens about it and that's the honest truth, so help me God. It don't seem nobody in this peaceful place could do such a rotten thing."

Getting to know more of Sheriff O'Hoolihan's background and future plans was helpful to me. In as this was for reasons I have yet to divulge, let us just say that the more I knew of this sheriff's past, the easier it would be for me to instigate certain plans of my own.

Therefore, during an "accidental" meeting with him on Love Lane, I learned that he had been a difficult child, was adopted three times, and that his second foster father was famous for lying. This man, Henry Hadwijch by name, had once been the sales representative for golf carts sold to prison inmates, or so he told everyone, always adding that he was also successful at selling lobster bibs to the prisoners. It became obvious to me that O'Hoolihan adored Henry and was completely taken in by the outlandish stories, even though his foster mother was always interrupting the tall tales by screaming, "For God's sake, Henry, quit telling the boy these ridiculous lies!"

Prior to Henry's death (nudist camp, lightning), many other people constantly told him to cease and desist. Even members of the Hadwijch tribe said that his lies were the most transparent they ever heard. Whenever anyone challenged him he always responded by saying, "Well, that's the truth, just as sure as I'm born, sure as June bugs in June. And that's the honest truth, so help me God!" But O'Hoolihan, dismayed by the reactions of his foster father's critics, was deeply entranced by the stories and believed each and every word.

According to our gullible sheriff, there were several other admirable things that Henry did. One was the fact that he occasionally wore his undershorts on the outside of his pants; another was that he could flip a lighted cigarette inside his mouth and blow smoke rings. O'Hoolihan's favorite was Henry's proud display of his superfluous third nipple.

Our sheriff was also mesmerized when hearing his foster father tell of his childhood experiences at grade school; the time he had to write "Spitballs are not free speech" one hundred times on the blackboard, which was followed the very next day by having to write "The principal's toupee is not a football."

It had become common knowledge that Henry firmly believed that the foul odor rising from the District of Columbia is not because it was built over a stagnant swamp, but simply because of the odoriferous politicians there. Henry loudly proclaimed his strong views, even though they were at odds with each other. He prided himself for being both an activist for lowering medical costs and a staunch advocate for increasing the price of prescription drugs. On the other hand, he could be quite single-minded when it came to controlling his libido. O'Hoolihan told me that he believed Henry to now be marching around in heaven with a sign that said, "I tried saltpeter and it not only worked but shriveled my fingers too."

So we could proceed with our plans. The quarry was a credulous, guileless, trustful boob. Excellent!

This information about Sheriff Oliver O'Hoolihan's background was intriguing, yet I held strong doubts as to the veracity of some of it. Punctuating other statements of his, the often repeated "so help me God" indicated a boyish tendency to exaggerate, if not tell outright lies. I could not help but wonder if he was as upset at not being able to solve the recent murder as he had seemed.

That O'Hoolihan had served time at Sing Sing was an established fact; that he openly admitted it was surprising to me at first, before being struck by his trusting, childlike nature. Exactly how he had been able to become a sheriff, even at a place where one was unapt to find dangerously illegal activity, was a puzzle I had yet to solve. Perhaps his crime had been one that the official who hired him could overlook with integrity, or possibly ignore. Of one thing I was certain, and it was that my "pal" was remarkably open when talking about himself. In fact, like many I have known, that was by far his favorite subject.

Chapter Two

During the following week I was astonished to learn that Mrs. Robey had invited Sheriff O'Hoolihan to give an hour-long cultural lecture at her library. Of all the locals he seemed to be the most culturally deprived and the least likely to be chosen to speak publicly on any subject, much less that of culture. I could not help but presume that the woman had mixed him up with someone else. However, as far as I knew, there was not a soul within twenty miles who could speak intelligently on that particular subject. Even though I usually made a point of avoiding community events, the sheriff's speaking engagement was certain to be an event not to be missed, and so, looking forward to being entertained by a farcical display of incomprehension, I attended the lecture.

It was hardly surprising to find that some rows of chairs in the library's reading room were all but empty. Mrs. Robey, dressed to kill—black feather boa, ebony broach, pointed witch hat—looked rather peeved that extra chairs had been brought in for nothing and her thin lips pouted as if she were a pampered child deprived of a lollipop. Sheriff O'Hoolihan, a sight to behold, had gotten himself up in a loose wide-striped outfit that was highly inappropriate for the occasion. He made the type of late entrance that is traditionally done for theatrical effect, although I am sure his was unintentional. When keeping an eye on the chairs so as not to bump into any, he tripped on the step up to an improvised speaker's platform, and again tripped on his untied shoelace, then fell flat on his face. This was just as entertaining as I had expected. When he began to speak, his voice sounded tentative but gained assurance as he progressed, the words increasing in volume and speed, a development which caused several nearby listeners to inch back their chairs. There were stark contrasts to his vocal range, the high tones sounding like the gravelly scraping of an automobile when the ignition key is turned on when the motor is already running, and his lower register was quite similar to the ominous rumblings of an approaching tornado. It soon became clear that his idea of a cultural talk was to tell us about deadly weapons, and he had set up a projector with which he planned to show the various types. Unfortunately, or probably not, he had forgotten to bring the slides, ones that showed his childhood peashooter, and his two revolvers named Lovey and Dovey, guns which he jocularly referred to as his twin doves of death. It was just as well that the projected images of these items were to be left to our imaginations. If memory serves, the words of his lecture went as follows:

Ladies and gentlemen and, er um, everybody else, you are all very welcome to this, uh . . . ahem . . . hour-long picture show. Without some pichures I can't give you a real, ummm, clear idea of deadly weapons. . . and the danger in them. And the fun in using them! Like what that mean old felon had when knocking off our poor little Shirley, all of which I couldn't give you any real clear idea of without opening this here pichure show without them pichures I done forgot. Anyways I, ahem, open it.

Well anyway, I'm sorry to say I've just about given up on finding out who little Shirley's killer is, and so I'm thinking if I can make money enough from culture talks like this I can leave here and buy me a ticket to New Zealand or some-place where I can feel I ain't lived in vain. I mean I don't wisht to go on living here in vain, see? I'd rather live in New Zealand, or even New York City if worst comes to worst. Hey, I wish them guys what built this liberry had put in more ventilation. Wouldn't you all agree it smells somewhat like feet? But if we ask nice maybe Miz Robey'll splurge on some Airwick or something.

Honest, I really don't care for money, so help me God. I just need it to travel round to see the world and buy me some new clothes. These here striped ones what I got on were a great success in Sing Sing. They came for free, but then how often does money ruin a guy. Me, I should like to be ruined, but then I may have to get along as I am.

Now as to culture like what Miz Robey says I'm sup-posed to talk about. Well folk—and this is the honest trut: I ain't so cultured, no real artist myself, but anyways I'm just nuts about pichures. Photographs of little girls shot through the head for instance. Some are very pretty, kinda sweet to look at for a short time and, as I said already, I like them. In fact I've always been nuts about them art-type pictures, and though I'm no painter myself, I could do graffiti at a very tender age. When little I once lived on a farm with my foster parents and covered the attic walls with suggestive stick figures. Chickens mounting other chickens and cows mounting other cows and stuff. Yeah, they really do when in heat. Anyways, my foster parents noticed them drawings and said I had a future before me, but up to that time I'd no idea it weren't behind me. Well, then time passed on. It always does. By the way, does any of you folks have the time? No? So then pretty soon I growed up to be a man, not much of an artist but I've been mixed up with art. I had an uncle who took snapshots of me with his Baby Brownie and I had a cellmate who took anything he could get his hands on. Haw haw haw! That was a good one! And then when I was on the run in Babylon, Babylon in Long Island, a famous artist wanted to paint me but I said nerts to that. I mean who wants to have to scrub all that paint off yourself? And next there was this old goat who wanted to sculpture my bust but I said I ain't got none and even took off my shirt to prove it. Well, never mind about that, it was the start of a whole nother story.

Mostly I go for the dramatic art, though I weren't much of an actor myself. It was at James F. Oyster Elementary School where I was to be featured in *The Ruins of Pompeii*. They dressed me up as a pile of rubble and I thought I was doing pretty good as a ruin till the teacher handed over my part to this other kid. It was kinda disappointing but then things turned out worse when I played the lead in *The Burning Mountain*. That was really not good. Admittedly, I was a dangerous Stromboli. Everything got out of hand and they had to call the fire department.

Well, now I think of it, such remembrances always makes me ask where are the pleasures of my youth? Hence arises a really touching question: where are the girls of my youth? Some are married and some would like to be. Oh, my Florrie! She went and got hitched to another. Good thing too. They often do. I hope she is happy because I am. Hey, I notice some of you folks are looking at your watches. Well, how's about it, won't nobody gimme the time?

As a prisoner I was much more successful than as an actor because us jailbirds wanted out and developed all kinds of nifty plans to achieve that goal. I got a pichure of the shovel what made my pal Silvester's escape possible. And there was the skeleton key mailed to me in a cake. Well, that dern key didn't work, no matter whichever way I turned it, right end in or otherwise. And the cake was stale and I went and broke a tooth on it. The big one right in front. Right there, see? I mean see where it was? My favorite of all these pichures is this one of myself.

Oh yeah, I shouldn't forget to tell you what I learned at Sing Sing. You know the difference between a prison cell and a house? Give up? Well, it's that you can lock your house from the inside. Haw haw haw! That was another good one, right? Anyways I was more successful as a prisoner than as an actor because they finally let me out for good behavior and, whatdaya know, here I am doing this culture talk for money.

Music is something else I also go for and involve myself with. Listening to myself sing makes me feel better. You can bet it's true what some writer guy once said about music being what shoos the savage beast. But I don't sing all that much, specially none of that hoity-toity opera stuff, but my yodeling usually got some swell compliments in the prison showers. It's Tarzan what inspires me. Yeah, I know this talk ain't had much to do with deadly weapons but . . . well, so what if I'm just talking about singing and acting and stuff. Lots of talks I've had the patience to sit through had nothin' to do with anything at all.

So then, just the other evening, some cute young guys came under my window and sang the carol "Come Where My Savior Lies Dreaming." But I didn't go down there. I wanted to but was afraid they'd think me fruity. By the way, if you want to know the honest truth, I like girls best mainly because I'm supposed to.

But more about music. I onest met a Mormon man in Utah who could play two Jew's harps at once, and he hadn't any teeth, not a tooth in his head, yet that man was married. He was married better than any man I ever met. His wives, too, only not so much as him. I remember one of his wives sang me the song "Sweet Angel, Do Not Fly Away" and I told her not to hold her breath.

"Uh oh, here I am talking culture and ain't even able to show you the slides of my twin doves of death. You'da been really taken by 'em. Oh, well. Hey can't nobody give me the correct time? It's gotta be an hour gone by now. Miz Robey, am I done yet?"

*

Later in his office, with his eyes fixed on a point somewhere just above my head, O'Hoolihan began to sing "Toot Toot Tootsie, Goodbye," making a shambles of the tune and also forgetting the words. He droned on in an unvarying tone, neither shout nor murmur but allied to both. When his song tapered down to a creaking halt he smiled bravely and I noticed the hint of tears at the rims of his pale blue eyes. "Why were you singing?" I inquired. "Well, pal, that's what I always do to cheer myself up," he replied.

"What seems to be the problem?"

"It's the same like what I said about Shirley at the library. I know my English ain't so hot and I ain't used to talking in public but that was a pretty good talk anyways, huh?"

"Well you certainly had my attention." It was best to be kind. "You still have found no clues to the killer's identity?"

"Nope, nothing at all and my dog ain't been no use either. Instead of helping me track the killer he just noses around in my office trash basket, removes stuff, and doesn't even put it back. What a mess, and the murderer's still at large and everything's really gotten me down. In fact I'm about to turn in my badge and move on to a job I'd be better at."

"Oh, really? I am so sorry to hear it." This was not a surprising turn of events. Likable though he was, if this muddle-headed sheriff gained a second brain he would be a halfwit. "What would you like your new occupation to be?"

"Well, I'm up for grabs; I mean I ain't quite decided yet." Removing several carefully folded sheets of paper from his back pocket, he shyly handed them to me and said, "Seeing how you got good English, I was thinking maybe you'd be so kind as to help me with these here job applications?"

Even though knowing that correcting the letters would likely be a rather time-consuming chore, I agreed to his request, took the pages home, sat down at my typewriter, and and read:

Dear Sirs

Inre ference to your ad posted at Purcyville's Do Drop Inn I wish to offer my services for the position of architectual draughtsman. Tho my previous training is in criminal justice I got my own ruler and am willing to move to your vasinity for a swell new career in draughting.

Dear Sirs

I am writing to answer as to your need for a flower arranger. Well I never done flowers before but I got experience in the gathering and placement of dice and am real eager to switch over.

Dear Sirs

I am writing this to offer myself in the position of a spanish speaking clerk with your outfit. Tho I dont speak spanish as such I can understand Tex Mex waitresses and will improve real fast. You can contak me at the return address on this here envelope.

Dear Sirs

I recently come upon your ad for the position of pet groomer. Well such as tick removal is just what I already do a lot of on my own dog and he sure would not mind if I practice the other stuff on him sos when you hire me I am sure to be a expert.

Applying correct usage to the sheriff's hopeless illiteracy would be more of a challenge than I had expected, but I was determined to help and continued to read:

. . . for the position in your brokerage business. Tho my extensive training is not in that partiqular field as such I am plenty qualified to break almost anything youd wish.

. . . position of body massaging. Well thas for sure right up my alley. My strong hands are really strong and good at rubbing any body, girls and guys in particular and I know some who would be sure to recommend my expertease if you ask them nice.

. . . copyreading. Well thas a job what will sure use my talent to the full. But if I deside to take it might you be so kind as to send me a weeks pay in advance? I would sure apreshiate it because it will help get me relocated in your location.

Transforming these hopeless job applications into correct usage would have been beyond the powers of the eminent stylist William Strunk but, more out of pity than with any expectation of being able to help, at least I was able to correct the spelling and punctuation, change his loopy scrawls into typed versions, and then return the letters to the sheriff for posting.

Two weeks later, I spotted O'Hoolihan trudging along Love Lane. His walk resembled that of people whose thighs are too big and give a childlike braced look as if they needed their feet to be wide apart lest they fall. His general appearance reminded me of his bat-eared mongrel dressed in a neatly pressed sheriff's uniform for a comic photograph. "Hey, pal, how's your hammer hangin'?" he roared on his approach. Ignoring this rather personal question, I inquired if there had been any answers to his applications. "You won't believe it but there ain't been any, not none at all," he replied. I would not have believed it if there had been any.

"Oh, really? I am sorry to hear it."

"I guess I must've been overqualified or something. But thanks for your good help in fixing up them letters anyways."

"What will you do now? Shall you be continuing your investigations or send out more applications to other places?"

"More letters, but first I gotta find out what kinda work I'm best at."

"That seems quite sensible. How will you obtain this knowledge?"

"Well, I got this great idea and I'm just on my way to Miz Robey's liberry to find out from one of them books on gaster. . . uh, that gastrolley thing."

"Do you mean astrology?"

"Yeah, that's it, gastronogy!"

"What is your sign?"

"Sign? I ain't intending to be no sandwich boarder."

"Your gastronogy"—he now had me doing it—"is based upon astrology, and the forming of one's horoscope is contingent to one of the twelve zodiacal representations. What is your date of birth?"

"Well, I'm pretty sure it's about nineteen twenty or so, but nobody ever told me the exact date. My first foster parents—there was a whole slew of 'em—had trouble remembering us kids' names, much less our birthdays. But I figure the Christmas presents I got for being a good kid must've been for my birthdays too, which likely means I was borned in December."

In his maturity he was still walking like a little boy, now rocking back and forth with one foot on the curb and the other in the street. "If memory serves, I believe the December representation is Capricorn the goat."

"Well, whatdya know. Hey, man, you got my goat! Ha ha ha! What a good one!"

These witticisms were best to ignore. "It just so happens that I have an astrological volume at home with an extensive chapter on the traits and aspects of Capricorns. If you like I can copy out this information for you—a simple matter that would be no trouble for me to do, and it would save you the bother of going to the library."

As I had expected, O'Hoolihan accepted my offer. However, I had not been altogether frank with him, in that there was no such volume in my possession. I preferred for the sheriff to remain in his current position; in fact it was imperative if my stay in Purceyville was to be successful. The horoscope that I prepared was a sham that might cause the gullible fellow to continue fumbling around for the killer after he read the following:

Capricorns like to keep their rooms tidy and hate disorder. Furniture, framed pictures, and even throw cushions angled wrong drive them insane. The nit-picking would be sickening to their friends if they had any. Numerous Capricorns have been ostracized for their excessive fastidiousness. They are cold, unfeeling, and often fall asleep while fornicating.

Certain Capricorns are at times artistically inclined but their vivid imaginations cause them to have difficulty with reality. They actually believe the ridiculous stories they tell, but everyone knows they are inveterate liars. Whenever they think they are being humorous everyone howls with discomfort.

Male Capricorns are extremely likely to be either homosexual or at least bisexual. The men are usually gigolos and the women are often prostitutes. Both have fair chances for employment and monetary gain, even though they expect too much for too little. Furthermore, their procurers usually rob them of whatever they earn. All working Capricorns eventually get venereal diseases and can be pederastic.

Although their intentions are often well-intentioned, they are inclined to be careless and forgetful. This causes them to make the same stupid mistakes over and over. Nobody can be blamed for thinking them to be totally mindless.

Occasionally Capricorns can be shrewd in their dealings with bill collectors and parole officers, but they cannot be trusted. They may, however, achieve a modicum of success because of their shameful lack of ethics.

Capricorns are ultra-conservative, fear taking risks, and tend to rely on their looks to compensate for having such limited talent. They are victims of self-enchantment, constantly kiss mirrors, yet they can be sympathetic to other people's deficiencies. It is an established fact that Capricorns are habitual apple-polishers.

There has never been a Capricorn of any importance. It is extremely unlikely that they will ever find legitimate work suitable to their limited capabilities, which is why they will always be applying for welfare and never be worth a wooden nickel. They should just give up and end it all, or else continue with their present occupations.

MICHAEL,
THE MEDIUM-SIZED BEE

Good folks, maybe there has been too much incongruity piling up, much too much conflict and seesawing feelings. What's needed here is something consistent, something in life that is as ever-present as death:

There was nobility to the final flight of Michael, a medium-sized bee. Having been sucked through the front grid of a speeding truck, then through its glove compartment, carburetor, differential, and other mysterious places, Michael was miraculously expelled from the tailpipe and thrown onto one of the piles of trash which so often border the Long Island Expressway at Sunnyside Boulevard, exit number 46.

After floating round and round in a rain-filled Dixie cup, he was lifted out and subjected to the indignities of artificial respiration. Yes, folks, a little kid pumped Michael's legs and poked on Michael's chest, and such a crying shame, you'll say, but better him than me, better Mike, who's born self-sufficient and can't understand that sort of stuff.

Well, back came Michael's strength!

And after shaking dry his wings, he spread them giddily, flew up a ways, then fell. On his back, and sensing some last undefined, not wholly understood final outrage, Mike jabbed his stinger every which way in vain, uncoiled his long lip at the world, doubled up, and died.

MY DEAR DOGMATIST

Believe it or not, Budd was a talking dog. In fact he had an amazing vocabulary and at times could get really philosophical. We often discussed religion, a subject that usually caused friction between us. Unlike myself, Budd believed in the existence of God. Most canines do. They gaze upward and howl to who they believe made the moon and the stars and everything. It's a doggie thing. In Budd's case, he usually got to his front knees at the foot of his bed, lifted his shaggy head, and thanked God for Frisbees, fire hydrants, touch-tone telephones, and anything else he felt worth howling about. Woo woo woo—I can almost hear him now. You probably think I'm kidding but it's the honest truth.

My Budd not only talked but was able to sing. His vocal range was amazing, almost glass-shattering. He was best at hymns. "A Mighty Fortress Is Our God" and Bach's

"Magnificat in D" were a couple of his favorites. Neighbors hardly ever complained.

Well, one of the many religious issues that Budd and I didn't see eye to eye on concerned furniture. He believed that God created the sofa especially for dogs. He was adamant about it and there was no use telling him to get the heck off. Lounging there for hours at a time, belly up with paws folded in contemplation, he counted his blessings and thanked the Almighty for making it possible to lead a dog's life.

And then there was the crotch business. You know how dogs are. Any old crotch will do. Turned out that Budd mixed up various odors with ecstatic religious experiences. Can you imagine! When I pointed out the social lapses occasioned by sniffing privates Budd replied, "Try it, you'll absolutely love it!" He even had a little doll made of dung to worship. When I mentioned that it seemed a bit unorthodox, he growled, "Nonsense! All you humans think graven images should only be made of wood or stone."

Anyway, when not lying around on the sofa, he spent a whole lot of time traveling to the Vatican, deepening his beliefs and looking forward to his eventual ascent to heaven. No one could convince him that God does not exist or that belief in an afterlife is just wishful thinking.

At one point, just before All Souls' Day, he started going on about spreading the word by becoming a missionary to China. I did not think that was such a hot idea. "How much do you know about saving souls?" I asked. "Plenty," he exclaimed. "I've read the glorious sermons of Aimee Semple McPherson." I guess he didn't know she was arrested for fraud.

By now it will come as no surprise to you that my pious dog was bound and determined to convert, not just me, but all sinners everywhere. Budd wasn't certifiably insane, mind you, certainly not a mad dog in the noonday sun. You wouldn't get rabies or the mad cow disease or anything like that. Just fleas. But disagree with him and it was bite bite bite. My butt would be sore for a week.

Towards the end of his life (Pope's blessing, epileptic fit), Budd developed a keen interest in money. He went around licking up to philanthropic foundations and arranged to have all the money in my bank account transferred to himself. When I demanded for him to put it back he explained that, since money is the root of all evil, he had burned it. Now I ask you, was that a nice doggie or what?

I should've traded Budd for a less obstreperous companion, one like my previous dog, Dee Dee. She was perfect, had no special talent or cockeyed concept of the hereafter. Her adoring eyes beamed and her long tail wagged whenever she looked at me. Budd's eyes were devilish and his pathetic little stump of a tail only vibrated when he saw me leave for work. Even so, I've got to admit that I miss him and our contentious spiritual discussions.

A week or two before Budd passed away he developed

mysterious red dots on his paws. The vet thought they were from scratching at fleas but I knew better—stigmata, a sign of religious ecstasy. Either that or of an unbalanced mind. When burying dear Budd next to Dee Dee in the pet cemetery I couldn't help but wonder if God existed after all, but then soon realized that the answer wouldn't change my life a bit. Earthly life is heaven enough and then it's just ashes to ashes and all that's left are the evergreen memories of those who were here.

ACKNOWLEDGMENTS

With deep gratitude to publisher Cecile Engel, advisor Robert Gottlieb, close reader Joseph Focarino, book designer Greg Mortimer, introducer Suzanne Carbonneau, and especially to my dance company's Executive Director John Tomlinson, whose watchful eye is always keeping me out of trouble. They made all of this possible.

A Note on the Type

This book was set in Fournier, a typeface made by Monotype in 1924. The design is based on types cut by Pierre Simon Fournier, circa 1742, some of the most influential designs of the eighteenth century. Fournier's types were among the earliest of the "transitional" style of typeface and are seen as a link to the more severe "modern" style made popular by Bodoni later in the century. They had more vertical emphasis than the old-style types, greater contrast between thick and thin strokes, and more subtle serifs. Fournier has a light, clean look on the page and is legible and elegant for text.

Designed and composed by Greg Mortimer

Printed and bound by R. R. Donnelley,
Harrisonburg, Virginia

So here cometh
"Delphinium Books"
To recognize excellence in writing
And bring it to the attention
Of the careful reader
Being a book of the heart
Wherein is an attempt to body forth
Ideas and ideals for the betterment
Of men, eke women
Who are preparing for life
By living. . . .

(In the manner of Elbert Hubbard,
          "White Hyacinths," 1907)